Dust Collector

KEVIN A. JOHNSON

Dust COLLECTOR

EXPERIENCING THE GOD WHO COLLECTS
WORTHLESS THINGS AND MAKES THEM
INTO GREAT THINGS IN HIS HANDS AND
FOR HIS PURPOSE

Providence House Publishers
WWW.PROVIDENCEHOUSE.COM
FRANKLIN, TENNESSEE

Copyright 2010 by Kevin A. Johnson

All rights reserved. Written permission must be secured from the publisher to use or reproduce any part of this book, except for brief quotations in critical reviews or articles.

Printed in the United States of America

14   13   12   11   10   1   2   3   4   5

Library of Congress Control Number: 2010922072

ISBN: 978-1-57736-426-9

Cover and page design by LeAnna Massingille

PROVIDENCE HOUSE PUBLISHERS
238 Seaboard Lane • Franklin, Tennessee 37067
www.providencehouse.com
800-321-5692

I wish to first and foremost dedicate this book to my Lord and Savior Jesus Christ, without whom the writing of this book would never have been possible. His revelation and spiritual influence has been painted all over the pages of this book. Finally, I wish to dedicate this book to the countless people out in the world and in the church, who have not yet looked into the mirror of God's true design and image for their lives. It is my passion, commitment, and hope that every human being on this planet would catch a glimpse of all the beauty of God that is laid up for the ugly ashes within their lives. Please know that only through contact with Jesus Christ can you truly come into the true image of exactly how you were meant to look.

CONTENTS

Preface	ix
The Junkyard: God's Favorite Place to Find Priceless Works of Art	1
Born Dirty	15
Never Too Dirty to Be Made Clean	25
Worthless Things Become Useful Things	33
Recycle It, Baby!	47
Only Those Who Are Not Afraid to Become Dust Carry God's Breath	57
Moving from Dust Form to Spirit Form	71
Ten Steps to Rising from Life's Ashes	83
Born Small, Designed to Be Great	101
Ruling over Dust, Breaking Ugly Addictions	111
God's Masterpiece: A Beautiful Picture of God Remaking You	125
About the Author	143

PREFACE

We live in a world filled with the voices of so many people crying out in pain and agony over having lost someone or something. Everywhere you turn, you can hear the tormented cry of people whose lives have been reduced to dust. You might just be one of these burdened and broken ones who has had your life's dreams and goals shattered into a million pieces. Maybe you were married for twenty years, only to witness those years of marital bliss reduced to common yard dust because of an unfaithful spouse. Maybe you have spent all your life waiting on your prince to come and sweep you off your feet; instead, all you have had were frogs—frogs who only used you for the beauty of your body but cared nothing for the beauty of your spirit. Or, maybe you have tried for that promotion at work, but you keep being overlooked. Now you feel as if you are getting too close to retirement for them to even consider you for advancement. Let us face it, right now you probably feel like useless dust.

One thing is certain in this life: every human being on this planet will, at one time or another, feel as if he or she has nothing of value to add to their surroundings or even to this present world. If the truth be told, even the greatest men and women in history have not always felt so great about themselves. This dust reality we all experience from time to time stems all the way back to the first man and woman in the Garden of Eden. You see, Adam and Eve were doing quite well and had so much value and potential, until they decided to eat from the Tree of the Knowledge of Good and Evil. Once they ate from that tree, biblical history reveals how God cursed them back to the dust from whence they came. Now, this dust experience did not just have to do with the end of human life, it also impacted the limited way in which human beings would live. This is why so many people are depressed. Many find themselves wasting their money and their life's savings, and thus are relegated to financial dust. Some waste the chances of walking with and knowing God, only to come to a deathbed experience full of regret after wasting all their earthly lives on dust and crying out to God to save them. There are many people who throw away their chances of finding God's chosen mate for them by chasing after the unfulfillment of multiple sexual relationships which amount to nothing.

Although some people create a life of nothing but dust for themselves, there are also those who have been the victims of others' dusty lives. Some women have been raped and are now on the verge of committing suicide because someone else had been sexually abused, developed a low way of thinking about himself, and decided to bring those women down to his dirt level. Then, there are those who have committed suicide because some people in their lives have made them feel like one hundred pounds of nothing but common yard dust. So many individuals in this life have had their hearts broken by others who have been physically, spiritually, and mentally broken. We must understand that one person's dust will inevitably become another person's blindness. People who have been damaged and led to believe that their lives will never be anything but dust will soon attempt to influence others to see themselves the same way. One of the reasons we do not develop any God-designed vision, or any vision at all, is because we hang out with people who believe in nothing, have no standards, godliness, or morality, and do not have any vision for their lives. Their dust ends up blinding us to the reality of who God has made us to be and to the potentially visionary lives we have within us. Have you ever stood right in the path of a huge dust storm? Unless you had a protective mask, you would inhale so much dust that your lungs would not be able to get oxygen and you would suffocate. Or, your eyes would become so filled with dust that it would damage your vision and you would become blind. These are the same results that could happen to us if we allow people into our lives who only have one plan in mind—to cover us in mounds of dust.

While I do believe that we can be affected and even harmed by the dust of another person, I also believe that many times we create our own dust storms that cause us to perish. Some of us, in haste to become married, have married people who have verbally or physically abused us. These kinds of abuse have raped us of all God-released passion within our lives and have so damaged our mind that suicide has seemed a better option than life. Then, there are those of us who have wasted so much money on parties and extravagant living that we have lost houses, friends, spouses, and jobs. This kind of out-of-control life has led us down a long and lonely road. Sometimes, we are the destroyers of our own relationship with God and our own lives. I wish for you to know that dust is everywhere! None of us, as long as we are on this earth, can escape this reality. However, by the power of the Holy Ghost within us, we can live above the dust and become something much more than we are now.

With that last statement in mind, I have awesome news for you! It does not matter how you came into a dust experience, you can overcome your situation by the power of God in Jesus Christ. We have constant access to a God who specializes in turning dust into beauty. This same God who, in the Garden of Eden, made dust into a living, breathing, thinking, worshipping, and ruling creature can do the same with the dusty parts of our lives that are harmful and destructive. He has the ability to take that dust of rape in our lives and make it a tool with which we can counsel others who have been raped. He is further able to take the dust of lost virginity and enable that person to teach others that virginity lost does not have to lead to a life of prostitution. God can take the dust of abortion and make a woman into a mother who not only takes care of her babies, but also opens up her home to adopting babies that would have been aborted. Oh, yes, indeed. God is in the business of breathing His life and His transforming power into common dirt. By His mighty Spirit, God can take the dust of adultery and make an adulterer desire only one spouse; he can then teach others that just because a marriage might have been broken, by His strength, it can be mended. God, if given the opportunity, can take the dust of murder and make a murderer the voice of His love right in the prison of that murderer's dust. God has the ability to take the dust of drug dealing and breathe into a life that becomes a witness to many young people of the dangers of illegal drugs. God can take the high school dropout and make him or her the college straight-A student. God can do anything with dust that it cannot do with itself.

The dust from which Adam was made was not special. It was common, dead, inactive, and empty. Yet, when God touched it and breathed into it, it became alive and full of

God's Spirit. This is what God deeply desires to do with our lives. God wants us to bring our dusty life of sin, failure, brokenness, and formlessness to Him, and give Him free reign to mold us into His image. When you and I give ourselves over to this great dust collector, everything that had no form within our lives suddenly begins to take beautiful shape. In addition, everything used by Satan to try and blind our vision will be blown away from our spiritual sight, and we will be able to see the path of God set for our victory. God loves to touch and shape dust! Who but God could take something as horrible as rape and make something beautiful with the shattered remains of that victim's life? Only God can! Therefore, before you and I try to collect our own dust and before we try to judge what God can and cannot use, we should simply present every negative dust particle to Him and allow Him the opportunity to use them in our lives. Do not be quick to throw out any experience in your life until God has touched it or breathed into it. You might be surprised to find that what we believe to be junk might just be the very things that God is planning to transform and use for His great purpose.

God knows how to recycle the useless dust and garbage in our lives into something worth looking at and listening to, into a source of godly inspiration. God can take a tragedy and make it into the transformative story of a lifetime. God loves to use dust in order to create wonderful things because dust does not speak back to Him while He is at work. Dust does not question why He is doing what He is doing; dust is very submissive; and dust is so unlikely to become anything of worth that reveals the true depth of God's miraculous power. Dust testifies to the God who takes the impossible and makes it possible. When you and I become like dust in the hands of our awesome God, we allow Him to work mighty miracles in our lives. If you want to have a life filled with God's miraculous presence, you must stop trying to be strong in and of yourself and stop trying to make yourself beautiful or great. Let God, the true Creator, make you the righteous and spirit-formed soul that you are designed by Him to become. Get out of His way and let Him receive the praise for transforming the alcoholic into a sober counselor, the sexual addict into a celibate person, and the victim into a victor.

I wish to encourage you never to quit on life just because of a little dust. If you have committed a sin that makes you unable to look at yourself in the mirror, do not quit. If you have given in to lust and then found out that you are pregnant, do not quit. If you are a preacher or singer for the Lord and have suffered a divorce, do not quit. You need to get alone with God and pour out your dust in repentance at His feet. Allow God the opportunity to forgive you and cleanse you completely. Please know and be persuaded that God loves when His children repent for the dust in their lives, not when His children give up or walk away from Him. Therefore, if we have committed dust violations, then we should own it by recognizing our wrong, confessing it to God, and then turning our faces away from such a sinful action. In Jesus Christ, you already have the spirit of God's form ready to make your dead dust into a living, spirit-formed life!

Now, this spirit-formed life will provide you with supernatural ability to face any future dust experiences such as weakness, sin, failure, fear, sickness, or worry, and allow you to rise above them every time. Nothing within this world system will be able to bring you back down to a life controlled and overpowered by dust.

the JUNKYARD

GOD'S FAVORITE PLACE TO FIND PRICELESS WORKS OF ART

Our very own personal life's junkyard is really God's most precious gold mine.

Before you decide to dismiss that memory of some hurt, pain, bad relationship, or terrible experience as nothing but garbage, commit it to God and allow Him to decide if that experience is bad for you or good for you. I am amazed how we as a people are so quick to throw out every event or relationship that has brought us deep pain. We believe the sooner we can forget or discard a feeling caused by a very bad experience, the quicker we can begin to heal and get over it. Now, sometimes this is a good thing to do, but sometimes it is not. You see, whether we are Christians or non-Christians, we all have a human tendency to quickly determine what things are merely garbage and not good for us. Instead of consulting God and allowing Him the opportunity to use our garbage or junk to benefit someone else, we decide that if it hurts, then it needs to be gotten rid of. Who among us likes to keep trash in our homes? How many of us like to live with garbage? I would think that the answer to these questions would be, "None of us." Now, as long as we live on this earth, junk is going to happen to our lives and within our lives. No matter how deeply rooted in the Holy Ghost we might be, we are going to make mistakes that will pile up just like unwanted garbage in our lives. In fact, no matter how much we strive to choose the right kinds of relationships, sometimes the false ones will still find their way into our lives. I want you to also realize that despite your attempts to train your children in the right and godly way, some of them might still go through periods of rebellion. Listen folks, junk is all around us, and we will face it at one time or another. For some of you, you might be healthy and full of energy, then all of a sudden, you might be hit with sickness. Oh yes! We live in a world filled with junk and junkyard experiences.

Although we live in this junkyard world, we have a God who uses these experiences in our lives to make us into pure gold. Only God has the ability to take the most ugly experience in life and turn it into the most beautiful example of His awesome truth. Oh yes, my friends, the things which you and I have called junk are the very things God uses to accomplish His purpose in this earth. God loves to walk through the junkyard of our mistakes, weaknesses, lack of vision, poor decisions, and wrong turns in order to find the positive in the midst of them all. As a matter of fact, the Bible reveals how God is able to take all of our life experiences and make them work for His total good. God is always at work collecting lives that have been scarred and rejected by other people, so that He might resurrect them in order to bring resurrection to others who are dead—spiritually and emotionally. Therefore, before you throw out what you consider worthless junk in your life, please allow God to breathe His life and vision into it and uncover a beautiful work, His spiritual art.

Have you ever noticed that when construction workers are first building a house, everything on that land seems to be torn apart and without order? First, the ground has been dug up. Then, dirt, stones, and steel are everywhere. Next, you witness wood laying all over the ground. In fact, you probably would not see anything worth buying on that piece of property. However, if you were to return later to this same messed up property, you would see a beautiful and finished house. Now, I wonder what would be running through your mind at this moment. Simply because something might appear to be a piece of trash or mere garbage, be careful to not allow your first sight to form your last opinion. As human beings, our first sight is usually wrong when we are dealing with things in this earth which God has intended to put to use. In fact, it is usually our first sight that gets us in trouble. Some of us have thrown out the right relationships because, at first glance, they appeared to be wrong for us. This nearly happened to my wife. When I had approached my wife some years ago to tell her I believed that God had given her to me for marriage, she looked at me with a first glance and did not believe that I was fit for her, or as she said, "You're not my type!" After God had a heart-to-heart talk with her, she took a second and longer look. It was then that she looked past what she considered junk and saw the husband that she had been praying for. If she had continued to see me as only unfit junk, she would probably have missed heaven's treasure and would have been miserable for a very long time. Some of you are miserable in your walk with God because you might have made the classic mistake of searching for hidden treasure with untrained and non-spiritual eyes. All you are able to see is what appears on the surface, and that appears to be junk to you.

The first junkyard of our lives can be termed No Place for God. Every Christian on earth has been at this place and every sinner is currently here. In fact, before we were born of God's beautiful Spirit, we were born in sin, separated from such a loving and beautiful God. Our lives were a mess! Think about how many foolish and regrettable mistakes we have made while living on this pile of junk. We probably wasted time, giving our minds over to every human lust and pleasure known to humankind. I know that I spent so much time chasing after sexual conquests instead of pursuing God's love and real affection. I chased after the wrong kinds of love until I was tired and out of spiritual breath. Now, I know that I am not the only one who can say that this was my reality! I believe that all of us can say that life without God's presence was a life without purpose and without benefit. Although this was our sad and misguided experience, God came down, breathed His beautiful Spirit into our worthless lives, and we became a work of art that causes people around us to say, "Wow!" Yes, indeed! God knows how to see past our junk and garbage. I truly thank God that He does not wait for us to become clean because a dirty nature cannot clean itself. God takes us at the garbage level and then changes our very nature into pure gold. Praise His holy and wonderful name!

Once we, by the power and life-changing nature of God's Spirit, have been removed from the junk heap of No Place for God, then many of us may experience the junk heap of Rejection. Before we are born of God, each of us has experienced rejection on some physical or mental level. In fact, even after we begin to walk with God, rejection is still possible.

Some of us know what it feels like to have been rejected or cast aside as worthless by a parent or spouse. This kind of rejection is crippling to the soul because it makes us feel as if we have no reason for living. Rejection is a garbage pile that stinks up potential. It causes us to believe that God has no place for us since even our parents or mates had no place for us. This kind of junk heap can lead us into deep depression because it makes us feel like we are nothing and that our voice does not matter. If you are sitting in a junk pile of rejection right now, be encouraged! God has a way of taking stones which builders have rejected and making them hold up the building. This is what the Bible speaks of concerning Jesus Christ. God used the most rejected man in earth's history and biblical history, Jesus Christ, to attract millions of rejected sinners back to His kingdom's protection. This is awesome! Your rejection is exactly what God will use to reach those more greatly rejected than you. Therefore, your personal rejection, although very painful, represents another person's acceptance. People like to know that another person has been where they are and has experienced the same pain. For some wonderful reason, this makes us feel more comfortable and encouraged while living on earth. The stench of your junk-filled rejection, once perfumed by God's breath, will become sweet aroma for change and deliverance on behalf of someone else.

There may be some of you who have fallen into the junkyard of a bitter or quiet divorce. Divorce is a very difficult process, and sometimes the stench of it can linger for five or ten years. At this present moment, you might feel like less of a preacher, singer, deacon, or child of God because of the situation. Whether your sin caused this divorce or your spouse's sin against you caused it, pain is still associated with it. Maybe people in your family or church have judged you and might not want anything to do with you. You might even be struggling with hating yourself. Regardless of your pain in this junkyard called Divorce, God will not run from you. You need to run to Him! God wants to get His eternity-sized hands on your life experiences and use them to encourage others who have also been broken in this way that they, too, can find victory. If you hand it over to our recycling God, He will take your failed marriage and minister healing and love to other marriages on the brink of divorce. With God's touch, your divorce garbage pile will become heaven's treasure of protection for another person's marriage.

Now, some of us might have beautiful aroma-filled marriages but a stinking pile called Financial Waste. Although some of us have not squandered a marriage, many of us have wasted our money. We live in a spend-spend world instead of a save-save world. Every time we turn on the television set, we see companies advertising to us and influencing us to spend more and save less. Let us face it! We live in a consumer-filled world. If we are not careful, it will cause us to use God's financial seed gift for our own greedy purposes. So many of us are living from paycheck to paycheck because we will not store up or save financial seed into God's kingdom, and we do not invest or save our money. As a result of this, we have no reserve cash in case something unexpected happens, and we end up spending the money that should have aided other believers, thus causing our own financial wells to dry up. If you are in this place of a lack of financial discipline, do not give up! Repent and let God touch your mind and pocket book. Let Him be God, not only in your head but also in your bank account. Then, He will wash you clean, by His power, make you financially stable, or even give you great wealth. He will show you hidden treasure lying beneath the junk of poverty within your life.

Maybe you find yourself in the junk heap of Crime and now you are behind prison bars. On the other hand, you might be an ex-offender or ex-prisoner. Then again, maybe your criminal offenses are less severe and you are on house arrest or doing community service. If any one of these realities fits you right now, I want to inform you that in Jesus Christ, you can be born free and live free. Perhaps you are wallowing in self-pity right now and feel as if you have no more life. Maybe you are contemplating suicide, and you cannot even look your family members in the eye. I have good news for you. God is able to make prisoners into preachers and change a prisoner's mindset into one of freedom and power. Take a look at what God does with the apostle Paul, even after Paul had been responsible for killing many Christians. God raised Paul up, gave him a new spirit, and used him to bring many sinners to the saving arms of a loving God. Now, the God who took the junkyard mess of Paul's life and turned him from a murderer into one who pointed the way to new life can certainly use you behind prison bars or on house arrest. God is always itching to make thieves into givers, murderers into healers, and sinners into saints!

Perhaps there are those of us who happen to be sitting in the junkyard of Time Has Passed Me By. This junkyard heap is the place of wonder. Perhaps for you it is wondering if you are too old to have that child. Or, maybe you are wondering if you will ever find God's Mister Right or Miss Right for you. Some of you might wonder whether you are too old to go back to college. Others of you might be thinking that maybe it is too late to start that business. Then, there are those of us who wonder if Jesus will return before we can know the feeling of watching our children birth other children. Sometimes we become concerned that it may be too late to begin preparing for retirement. Then, there are many who are wondering if it is too late to allow God's Spirit to use us in that spiritual gift or ministry. Although this is at times a very scary junkyard experience, it is very necessary. God uses this feeling of anxiety to keep us on time with His vision or personal goals for our lives. This experience acts like adrenaline in the human body. Like adrenaline, it pumps us up to accomplish things that would seem too difficult for us to do under normal circumstances. Therefore, God uses our concern to prevent us from taking for granted and wasting the precious gift of time which He has given us. Do not be afraid of this feeling. While it might appear to be of no value to your life, you need these thoughts constantly lurking in the back of your mind to keep you focused on that which God has placed in front of you. Once again, God comes down to our junkyards in an attempt to find and manufacture a priceless work of art.

Well, have you had enough junkyard experiences yet? After getting all this good news thus far, I did not think that you would be getting tired anytime soon! As we venture further into the truth concerning God's love for spending time in the junkyard experiences of our lives, we find yet another experience which we must face. It is the Less Than Nothing junkyard heap. Every one of us has visited this place at one time or another. No one likes to be placed in a position that makes us feel small and insignificant. However, as long as God is making beauty out of ugliness, you and I will have to walk through this garbage pile of junk. If you are wondering how God can make us great while allowing us to become very small, the answer is more simple than you think. In order for God to use any vessel greatly, He must allow life's hardships, trials, failures, and weaknesses to make that vessel small. God will not use vessels until they have made God big in their mind and have made themselves small. God wants people who will lift Him up far greater than themselves. In order to make or fashion such people, He must allow them to be thrown onto the junk pile of less, small, and insignificant. Since the smaller you become determines how much greater God will use you, it is to your benefit to visit the junk heap of Less Than Nothing. Your greatest miracle, blessing, or movement of God can only happen when you have been less dependent on you and more dependent on God. In fact, according to the Bible, John the Baptist realized that he had to become small so that Jesus Christ could become big. You must understand that it is the same way today! We must die so that the resurrection power of God and sickness-healing glory of God can be manifested to those who have not yet believed.

I hope by now you realize that God is far more superior in making great vessels than anyone or anything. However, just give God any dead, old, decaying, and deformed thing, and He will make it into something very much alive, new, growing, and perfectly formed. God picks potentially great people out of the junkyards of their lives, and causes them to be far different from the place from which they came. This is so radical! Therefore, before you are too quick to give up on yourself, give your failures, mistakes, faults, and doubts over to God, and then watch with awe as He gives you a new you.

I know that there are people in your life who have already condemned you to failure. They have already given up on you becoming anything of value or worth. As a matter of fact, some of them have even told you to your face that your father was nothing and you are going to be the same. You do not have to live under the influence of your father's or mother's demons. Just because your father might have been an alcoholic does not mean that you are one step closer to the bottle. Just because your mother suffered a nervous breakdown does not have to mean that you are one wrong thought away from losing your mind. Please do not believe that just because you may have been sexually abused by someone in your family, you are destined to live like a victim—broken and never mended. That is not true! The Holy Ghost wishes for you to be encouraged in the following revelation: whatever God has allowed to take place in your or your family's life, He did so in order to have many junkyards from which He can miraculously pull spirit-filled and empowered vessels that will change their world. Therefore, count yourself as one of the blessed ones. You see, where sin greatly exists, God must pour out much more of His grace and His miraculous presence right there. This means that the worse the junk in your life gets, the greater God will be attracted to your vicinity in order to choose, call, and make you into something far better than the junkyard in which He has found you. What wonderful news! The greater the junk in your life, the greater the manifestation of the beauty and power of Jesus Christ within your life.

born
DIRTY

*The dirt in our lives did not just magically
appear; we were born with it!*

One day, a ten-year-old boy named Sam wandered into a small convenience store. As he moved through the aisles, his eyes became fixed on a watch. He wanted that watch so badly that, while the store manager's eyes had turned away, he grabbed the watch and ran out of the store as if he were a speeding bullet. When Sam got home, his mother immediately noticed the watch and confronted her son. After Sam told his mother that he had stolen the watch, she asked, "Why did you do it, baby?" Hoping that he would say that some friends made him do it, Sam's mother paused to listen to his answer. Sam then replied, "No one made me take the watch! I just looked at it and something within me knew that I was going to carry this watch home with me today."

From this story, we can see that there is a little Sam within each of us telling us that we cannot always avoid doing the wrong thing. The Bible calls this the inborn sin nature. In fact, after King David had sinned by sleeping with another man's wife and then arranging for that man to be killed in battle, he confessed to God in one of the biblical Psalms that he was born wicked. Actually, we were all born with a very serious birth defect that has nothing to do with any physical deformity. You see, if that defect were merely a physical stigma, then we could find a scientific way to remove it and live more productive lives. However, because that defect in the entire human race is spiritual, only God is powerful enough to remove it from our lives. Only God, through Jesus Christ, can fix what is wrong with us!

While it is clear that we were born dirty, it should also be very clear that because of Jesus Christ, we do not have to live dirty lives. However, it is very important for us to know the reality of the unholy and dirty ground from whence we were born. Although Jesus has now made us clean and is constantly making us beautiful, we must recognize that the very dark and dirt-filled nature will continue to try and make an ugly appearance, right in the midst of God's work within us. We should never think for one minute that this dirt is simply going to wash away without a fight. Dirt is going to fight us every day that we live, so we must realize that it is present with us, even though we do not have to become dirty because of it. In the New Testament letter of Romans, chapter 7, the apostle Paul revealed to that church that they would continually struggle with who they once were. He was informing them that they could not afford to be careless in their new spirit-formed lives by forgetting that there was an ugly, deformed, flesh-life still trying to control them through sin. This same message holds true for us today! We must understand that there is a real boogyman stalking us, and he is not a ghost or some character of myth or legend. This boogyman is the sum total of all the seeds of all the wicked thoughts, behaviors, and desires of our past sinful and dirt-laced existence. This very dirty figure attempts to haunt God's purpose, power, and character in our lives, hoping to bring us back down to our pit of dust.

There are many different ways this dirt will attempt to resurface in your new Spirit-born lives and overshadow any destiny of God for your life. For example, if you have finally found your prince, after years of waiting on God, you must be on the lookout for dirt. While it is a very pure thing to wait, saving yourself and your virginity for God's mate for your life, you should know that there is a strategy against both of you that would steal your virginity long before the blessed marriage has been sealed. The temptation exists to sample the forbidden fruit. In fact, the closer you and your future mate become, the more you will naturally want to take this introductory intimacy to the next level. Just because you both are attending church and studying the Bible together does not mean that you will be able to avoid this temptation. You had better know that around every corner in your preparation for marriage, dust is piled up and waiting to blow all over your potentially beautiful day of marital covenant. Because of this, you must be on guard at all times. In order to ensure that you do not experience a dusty night before your lovely God-breathed wedding day, you and your future mate have to spend more time in God's presence than in each other's. Think about it! You are going to have a lot of time with each other, so why not plant a first seed of time with God before your marriage? Practically speaking, you will want to spend time apart from each other, studying the Bible, fasting, and praying. These actions will honor God and will keep your focus on all things pure.

Perhaps you are not about to be married anytime soon, but you are a single Christian trying to hold on to the virginity which God has given you. For every single guy or girl trying to hold on to this purity, there are approximately ten single guys and girls who have already lost theirs and will try to convince you that you are weird or soft. As a matter of fact, in today's world, there is a generation of young people who make sex seem as if it were the greatest experience on this planet. Every day, you are going to be in classes with them, in church with them, and in neighborhoods filled with them. They are going to be used by Satan to entice the inner, dirty side of you to come out and play. There is a natural, God-given sensual side within each of us, but it has been perverted and twisted by our sin nature. Therefore, although the nature of God in you says to wait until marriage to have sex, that lustful image within you says to try it just once. Even now, you may be hearing inner voices saying things like: *You do not have to wait! You are going to hurt yourself if you wait! Everyone else is doing it, why not you? Your friends all think that you are a wimp!* Or, *God gave you a sex drive, use it!* You had better not allow the genie out of the lamp by giving into any of these suggestions. Once dirt is given any room in our lives, it will always multiply into a far greater mess than we expect. In addition, it will show itself to everyone else in our life's space.

Another area where dust would like to settle in our lives is found in what we allow in through our ears and eyes, whether it be music, movies, or television. Because of our sin nature, we all have ears and eyes prone to want to hear and see things that promote sensuality. I am a living witness that no matter how saved or spiritually deep we might be, if we allow sexually explicit movies to enter our hearing and vision, we could easily be led away to do some very raunchy things. Some years ago, while I was on a preaching mission in the United States I gave in to the curiosity and lust of my fleshy mind and watched very sexually charged movies. Now, I knew that this was wrong. However, since I could not experience sexual contact with my wife because she was still home in the Bahamas, I thought that seeing the act would be okay and make me feel less alone. I was stupid and dead wrong! This was not okay, and for years I lived with a struggle of lust in my life as a consequence of this action. What I thought was a one-time action almost caused me to lose my relationship with God and my holy and pure intimacy with my wife. The heat was pouring on me, and only by God's Holy Spirit was I able to break that cycle. You see, I had gotten into this kind of dirt because I had underestimated the power of past dirt to be resurrected in my life. If you underestimate that, you could find yourself as I did, splashing around in the mud produced by the dirt of a once-in-control sinful nature.

As Christians, we cannot afford to live in a state of denial. We must see that although Jesus has given us a new, spiritually-transformed birthmark, we still have to fight against our sinful and decaying flesh. We are not in heaven yet. What makes this fight so much more difficult is the reality that the inner man of sin has been around for a long time. We are warring against a mindset of sin that has been passed down from Adam and Eve, through thousands of generations, to us. Please note that when Adam and Eve sinned, according to the Bible, they passed along to every human being an ability to rebel against any and all laws or promptings of God. Therefore, the capability of human beings to sin began a long time ago, and in every generation, it becomes increasingly stronger to break and dominate. The longer sin is allowed to exist or to operate, the harder it will be to break!

Now, we as Christians in today's world are not just battling the nature or ability to sin passed down to us from Adam and Eve, but we are also battling every weakness, demon, failure, sabotage, and sin passed into our world by our very own father and mother. This is a very serious reality! This means that our fight becomes increasingly difficult, as those in previous generations had become increasingly worn down and weakened by a heavy and old dirt nature. This also means that we need to be more aware and awake concerning the operation of this dirt birth. We, in the Holy Spirit, can win every time as long as we never stop using the awesome weapons of the Spirit of God to blow away this old sinful dirt man opposing us.

As you continue the fight for freedom, you must never give up nor give into the inner suggestions of lust being fed to your mind. As an illustration, you might find yourself up for a promotion one day—a promotion you have been waiting and praying for many years. Now, this promotion should be fairly easy for you since you are always on time, you have a wonderful God-fearing attitude, you have been consistent, and you are well-qualified. You say to yourself, *This promotion is mine!* While you are very confident that they are already putting your name and title on the office door, you find out that Susan the newcomer has been chosen over you. Now, of course, you know that you are a child of God and that you should be happy for Susan, but then you hear a different voice speaking hate and disdain for Susan. This voice is your flesh, attempting to get you to lose a spiritual position as well as a physical one. Any one of us, at any time in this life, may be cheated out of a job, a house, or even a promotion. However, what matters most to God is not the job, house, or the promotion we may have lost but that we do not lose the influence of spirit birth in the face of dirt birth. Satan, on the other hand, would love for us to walk in the attitude of that dirt birth, thus giving place to his unholy agenda. He would love nothing more than for us to respond in sin, preventing sinners from seeing the beautiful nature of God within us. If sinners cannot see God's beauty within us, then they might believe that change is not possible. Listen, we will either be God's proof that His life is real, or we will be agents of Satan, proving that the sinful dirt nature rules.

I would further like to encourage you to be very watchful of the allure of the sinful dirt birth. This dirt happens to be very sneaky. It will always strike when we are least aware. In these dangerous times, this defective birth nature will strike right after you have had some great success due to your excellence on a job, in school, or on behalf of God's kingdom. It might be that you recently got a promotion at work or you might have just made all As in school. Maybe you just preached or sang at a conference where many people received Jesus Christ as Lord and Savior. It is at this very instant of joy and celebration, the moment that you are most vulnerable, that your dirt birth tends to show itself. During your celebration, your dirt birth will tempt you into thinking that your success is all because of you and that you are better than everyone else. As a result, pride begins to build within your mind; if you are not aware of this silent and secret pride, you will become heady and egotistical. This is why so many truly called and awesomely gifted men and women of God have fallen from grace and right into the deceptive arms of a sinful and arrogant lifestyle.

Think about it! Adam and Eve fell in this same way: their very own ability to rule the earth became the very rule that assisted in their fall from God's grace. Adam and Eve thought that because they had been given authority from God to have dominion over earth, they could change the game by making a cursed tree one that would be a blessed tree for them. Therefore, instead of listening to God's voice, they ate from the tree and changed the image of spirit into one of common dust. Afterward, God sentenced them back to the very dust that they had once been. Their reliance on their own ability to rule caused them to be ruled by the dust from which they had come. The reality of this story of Adam and Eve's fall is that a dirt birth can only produce a dirt end! Unless God by His living Spirit collects it and breathes into it, dirt can only be dirt.

Listen, keep a keen spiritual eye on your dirt birth. Let us keep it right where it belongs—under your feet. Realize that God has raised you up from your dirt birth and dirt end to give you a future filled with His power and divine nature—both results of His awesome breath. You must fight against this dirt birth, but you do not ever have to live six feet under the control of it! You were not designed by God to live beneath dirt but to live in the Heavens of God. You have been given a living and resurrected spirit that only knows how to live and soar as an eagle, far above the sinful and demonic dust storms below. Therefore, live high, live strong, live free, and most important, live like dust no more.

NEVER *too* Dirty to BE **made** *Clean*

A little dirt on a silver cup does not mean that the silver is worth any less!

"Oops!" This is probably the most common expression that you and I will hear as we travel through this earth. This expression is so constant and common because all of us, at one time or another, make some foolish mistakes. Now, we may not make all of our mistakes intentionally, but they will be mistakes, no doubt, and may have painful consequences. We all must understand that our human sin nature determines that at any given moment, we could find ourselves staring into the face of an "Oops!" It does not matter how deep we are in God or how deep we are in sin. The proof of life is that we are going to fall, either because of character flaws or because of a lack of godly character or human ethics and morals. Remember, we were all born dirty, locked up in the state of sin, and separated from God and His awesome cleansing righteousness. This reality suggests to us that if we were born dirty, then at some point, we are going to produce dirt.

Now, please know that no matter the size of your "Oops," the power of the cleansing blood of Jesus Christ and the presence of His cleansing Holy Spirit can make you clean. Oh, believe this truth. The only way that people in this life might not ever be made clean would be because these people love dirt so much that they ignore the reality that they are in need of cleansing. It is certainly not due to a lack of God's power. Then there are some who love this filthy, sinful world system so much that they live in constant blasphemy against the voice of the Holy Spirit and the calling of God. However, for those of us who desire to be clean from our dirt birth, please know that you and I are never too dirty that we cannot be made clean.

Perhaps you think that you have committed some terrible sin—one from which you believe you could never be forgiven by God or people around you. However, I want you to know that although some people may hate you until you die because of some crime or sin that you might have done, God is waiting with open arms to take your messed-up, dust-filled life and breathe into it His life. God loves people despite the most disgusting dirt within their lives, while people cannot even stand the sight of the dirt. He loves to take people whom the world pushes aside and considers too immoral or dirty and transform them into people who have the spiritual power to change the very world which previously hated and rejected them.

Are you still having difficulty in believing that God can do all of this? Well, doubt no more! As human beings, we are prone to believe that once people have become so filthy and dirty in sin, they can never be made clean. We think that there are certain mistakes which render a person non-redeemable. While the world says that you or I might be non-redeemable, we need to focus on what God says about us. God speaks the most beautiful words about the ugliest, broken lives. Only God can look at a man named Saul, a mass murderer of Christians in the New Testament, and say that he would be used to win many people to God's kingdom. Can you believe that? God sends a prophet to Saul and tells him that he would be changed from a killer to one who will point people to Jesus Christ, the giver of life. This is awesome! Who else but God can take a man named Moses, who had killed an Egyptian overlord, and use him to bring about the greatest exodus of refugees ever recorded in history? All throughout the Bible, we find that God constantly chooses people who have been written off as worthless, too ungodly, and too weak. He has cleansed them of their dirt, given them His strength, and used them to bring about the most miraculous movements on this earth.

What is the greatest sin in your life or your most terrifying secret shame that has you convinced that God is finished with you or that He would not touch you with a ten-foot pole? I tell you this: unless you completely blaspheme (speak wickedly) against the Holy Ghost, you can be made clean! Yes, indeed! God is waiting on you to seek Him and ask Him to touch you with His dirt-cleansing hands. Maybe you have just aborted a precious life growing within you—one that did not threaten your life—and now you are feeling guilty and depressed. Before you are deceived by Satan to kill yourself because of it, please drop that razor blade and know that God is waiting to save your life, even though you have killed the life of God's fetus. Once you come to Him in humility and sorrow because of your sin, God is able to wash off your sin dirt and make you a spokeswoman to women contemplating the same procedure. Do you think that because this sin is so great, God no longer sees your life as valuable? The answer to this question is, "Of course not!" God despises the murder of any life, whether that life be in the womb or outside of the womb, but He still loves all lives.

Furthermore, you might be a saved but convicted prisoner in jail right now. I wish to inform you that if you have committed murder, rape, child molestation, or any other crime in your past, once you have received Jesus Christ as Savior, you are a new creature. This means that in God's eyes, you are no longer a murderer, rapist, child molester, or criminal. However, in the eyes of many people, you are still all of these things and you are viewed as not worthy of life. Now, you cannot hate people for still seeing you and treating you this way. After all, you did do the crime, and you should be punished in accordance with the law. However, do not allow their hatred of you to make you believe that your salvation in God is not real or that God hates you—He loves you! Once you have been changed by His Holy Spirit, He is going to work on your life until He has made you a witness of how He is able to clean any life and transform any decaying soul that would trust Him to breathe on it such a great salvation.

As another example, maybe you have been married for ten years, and in one night you threw away this sacred covenant of marriage by having sex with a person in your office. After you confessed this indiscretion to your spouse, your marriage fell apart and you are now broken because of this. The worst part about all of this is that you are a God-called, chosen, and very influential pastor in your city. You then decided to bring this before the church and to step down as pastor of the ministry. This is not how you wanted your ministry or your marriage to end. You are hurting from all sides, and you are silently wondering if you will ever recover from this unholy mess. Well, I will say to you that one sin or one mistake does not have to mean that all the years of your ministry and marital life have no value. Once you humble yourself and repent before God, your mate, and the congregation, God is able to love you right in the dirt and mud of your present life's dilemma. God is then able to wash you afresh and transfer His miraculous life-transforming power over to you and revive His ministry in your life.

Do you remember Samson? Samson had disobeyed God, lost his eyesight, and had become the prisoner of the Philistines—God's mortal enemy. Samson knew that he was in a mess and that he had badly failed in the assignment God had given him, yet he looked up to heaven, repented before our great God, and asked God to give him His power once more. You see, Samson knew he had started wrong, but he wanted to finish right! Well, God did give Samson more power and Samson was able to bring a huge building down on the heads of the Philistines. Samson killed more Philistines in death than he had in all his life. You can do the same! God can use this dirt and death experience from which you are suffering. He can draw you back to Himself and then raise you up stronger and with greater spiritual revelation in order to teach and train many more Christians. Thus, your dirt can be used as an example to many that, while they may fall down into the dirt and muck of sin, they do not have to stay there nor die there. They can rise up by God's power and in God's power. Through confession and repentance, God can make you clean and can raise you up.

I hear you saying that you have done something more sinful or vile than any of the examples I have listed. You are a person who has walked with God from childhood and well into your adult life, but you have allowed the dirt of this world's pleasure and lust to creep back into your God-given pure life. Your great oops is that you have backslid. Do you think that there is really no way back to God? God has the power to bring back every person who wants to truly believe again. Before you backslid, the faith that was once given to you had created in you a living spirit that knows how to find its way back to God. Oh yes! Did you know that the living spirit within you has a homing beacon, just in case you get lost, that you can use to find your way back into the presence of God? Did you also know that God does not ever make anything unless He has already made a way for that thing to be repaired, transformed, or redeemed should it become damaged, dirty, or lost? Therefore, you can come back! There is a way back to God for the backslider. All the backslider has to do is follow the inner beacon voice of God's Spirit. Hear that voice and confess your backsliding, turn from the things which led you into this dark and dirty wilderness away from God, and then get back into a Spirit-filled and empowered Christian fellowship so that you can begin to grow again. Now, according to the Bible, if God still has a plan for His first chosen people (Israel), then you know that God still has a plan for your life. When God calls and chooses any people, He stays true to His intentions and plans for them even if they have never stayed true to Him and His purpose. What a truly awesome God! That is why there is no other like Him!

Well, I hope by now you realize that God has the power to clean every scrap of dirt in your life, and that you are never too dirty to be made clean. God is constantly finding ways to transform our dirt into something He can breathe into, form, and use to birth His spiritual life. God hates dirt, but He loves what He can make it into. He also loves that an imperfect vessel can be used perfectly to show His powerful might. Therefore, when God takes the dust of your life, transforms it into a greater form, and then speaks, sings, preaches, or works miracles through it, people begin to take notice. They begin to believe that He is real and that they truly need Him to change their formless, lifeless, and dirt-filled existence. It is at this moment that even an atheist would be comforted in knowing that there exists a cleansing and a Cleanser for his or her dirt. This Cleanser is none other than our one and only Living God!

4
Worthless THINGS BECOME Useful THINGS

Things that appear worthless to us are more useful to God. Be careful, then, not to quickly dismiss your life as worthless. God can give your life great worth!

It is always fascinating to me how, as human beings, we are so quick to dismiss many things in our lives as having no worth. We are so quick to label something or someone as worthless simply because they do not operate or look the way we think they should. In fact, we even grade people in our lives in this way, and we throw away good and God-ordained fellowship with other Christians because they might not dress the way we like or they might not act in a manner of which we approve. As a result, we cast them out of our lives as having no real worth to our spiritual growth and development. Sometimes we end up tossing out the people whom God has chosen to help us mature in the things of the Holy Spirit, simply because we never took the time to ask God why these funny-dressing, loud, and overzealous individuals were placed in our path. Since it is a fact that we do not know, see, or understand like God, it is very important for us to ask Him through much prayer and fasting to reveal the things, people, and situations that truly have great worth in our lives.

Some of the worst things that have happened to us, if we were to truly look back in our lives, have turned out to be those things that have made us stronger in faith or have pushed us to seek God much more. We are going to face some very scary and horrific things in this world. These painful situations, which seem of no benefit to us, are exactly what we need to increase, prosper, and walk in a God-driven life. You can also look at this from the perspective of your human body. Sure, when you look at your body, there are some funny-looking and even funny-shaped parts that you would say have no real worth. Your pinky toe does not look like a body part that, if it were removed, would cause you any sleepless nights, does it? However, if you were to go ahead and remove your funny-looking pinky toe, you would realize that it helped with your balance and was more important than it looked. In the same way, many things and people in our lives are more important and have a greater usefulness than we first assume or give them credit for. Therefore, before you neatly pack stuff up and throw it away, check with the God who made that stuff. You might be very surprised at what He will instruct you to keep. What might be even more surprising to you are the things that God might just ask you to endure.

Greatly used vessels of God are instructed and expected by God to go through the most worthless-looking experiences. If you want to be involved in any great movement of God on this earth, you are going to be required to go through some very crazy-looking processes. God uses what appear to be worthless obstacle courses to train His most successful soldiers. Therefore, I have one question for you. Are you prepared to sit in the classroom of worthlessness in order to become useful? I do hope that your answer is a resounding, "Yes!" Now, I want you to know that you are not the only one that God treats in this manner. Throughout the Bible, God required the people He called to participate in the worthless-looking stuff. In fact, in the biblical story of the wall of Jericho, God required His people to march around the city seven times, blow trumpets, shout, and break clay drinking vessels in order to experience one of the greatest battle victories of all time. Can you believe this? A simple march, trumpet noise, shouting, and smashing clay bottles was all that it took to get God's angels to move and destroy the strongest wall of that day. After reading about this story, I am prepared to do whatever foolish and worthless-looking thing that God might ask of me. Another truth this story reveals is that the more extreme the foolishness or worthlessness appears, the greater the victory will be at the outcome. Thus, when God tells you to go down to the dock and take your mortgage money from the first fish's mouth that you catch, like Jesus told one of His disciples to do, you better run down there and prepare to go fishing. I do believe that in these prophetically charged end times, God is going to ask us to take some crazy-looking actions. I also believe that if we trust in Him to do them, we will be profoundly blessed, and sinners will be greatly saved by the signs and wonders that shall be manifested through our obedience.

I am going to share with you several different scenarios that might possibly happen in your life or that God might require you to experience on behalf of His kingdom. In fact, you might just be going through one or maybe even all of them at this present time. If this happens to be the case, I pray that you will be inspired to allow God to turn each of the seemingly worthless situations in your present walk with Him into very useful tools of inspiration and exaltation.

In this first scenario, you are a very productive worker, making one hundred thousand dollars per year. You hear God telling you to leave your very lucrative job, take a one-year sabbatical, and spend time in India. Now, right away the first thought that might run through your mind is, *This is stupid! God. You are not stupid so this is not You talking to me!* Your little human brain cannot even begin to understand why this is necessary or even if it is really worth it. Therefore, although this looks worthless to you, God sees great worth in this. He knows that you have the heart for mission work because He gave it to you. What you do not know, but what God has already known, is that the orphanage in India where He would be sending you needs help from someone such as yourself who has a special anointing or empowerment from God for this particular kind of ministry work. Therefore, what seems worthless to you is really beneficial to hundreds of poor children in India and will give you the opportunity to be more fulfilled than you have been in years. If this scenario, or one like it, fits you, obey God and watch lives around the world be changed.

Maybe you are about to earn your bachelor of arts degree from a very notable college. Next you intend to further your education by going for a prestigious master's degree. However, as soon as you begin making plans to further your education,

God tells you to drop that endeavor, move back to your home state, and spend time doing social work in the poor and run-down inner-city neighborhoods. Of course this sounds completely off base to you and your plans that in the next three years, after getting your master's degree in psychology, you could very well be making approximately sixty thousand dollars per year working for a very lucrative firm. Since you are looking at the situation through merely human eyesight, it makes no sense. However, please take a look at what God sees and why He might be asking you to make such a sacrifice.

God, in His awesome foreknowledge and keen ability to plan your life years ahead of where it presently exists, knows that once you were to enter the inner city, His charisma and glory upon your life would help to rescue thousands of teens from suicide attempts. God also knows that the supernaturally charged program that He would develop through you would help hundreds of young women who would have gotten pregnant, avoid the kinds of promiscuity and illicit sexual behavior that would have caused the potential pregnancies. Therefore, although the money you would be making would be very small when compared to the sixty thousand dollars you would be giving up, the thousands of lives that God would use your life to save from hell, suicide, gun violence, gang violence, and AIDS would make you the richest person on the planet. Thus, whenever God asks us to do something that looks worthless, chances are there are countless lives at risk, and God is trying to use us to bring them His brand of eternal hope and salvation. Please be mindful that the bottom line with God is not money, but lives. And, when God wishes to rescue any life, He will sometimes require us to do things that appear worthless, stupid, and irrational to the human vision and mind.

Well, let us dig a bit more into other possible and worthless-looking assignments which God might ask us to carry out because He knows they have true value and usefulness to His purpose. We must keep in mind that God does not make any mistakes! Therefore, if you and I know this, we should have no trouble trusting that whatever He asks us to accomplish will be of the greatest importance to His kingdom. With all of that said, maybe you have never been sick one day in your entire life walk with God. All of a sudden, while getting a routine checkup at the doctor's office, a lump in your right breast is discovered. Later on, in that very same week, your doctor calls you at work and informs you that the lump is cancer. Suddenly, your heart begins to pound as if it were about to explode within your chest. You ask your doctor how this is possible since no woman in your family's history has ever been afflicted with breast cancer. He then tells you that sometimes it happens and that you should begin preparation for treatment.

When you arrive home after work, you run straight into your bedroom and begin to cry out to your God. You wait to hear what God has to say concerning the cancer and hope that He would immediately remove this vile thing from your body. God does speak to you and informs you that His grace is enough and that He wants you to go through the fight of this cancer without Him quickly, supernaturally removing it. At first, you begin to wonder why God would be so hard and uncaring concerning your condition. You are dumbfounded as to how God, your Healer, could justify allowing you to endure this massive struggle without lending you the assistance of His awesome healing hands. While thinking these thoughts, the truth hits you like a ton of bricks. You recall how in the New Testament, an apostle named Paul had asked God to remove a thorn in his side. You further recall that God told him that He would not remove it, but that His grace would be enough. Once you are encouraged by this scriptural truth, you are all set to be God's witness. God is not only able to cure any disease known to humankind, but He is also powerful enough to allow His children to endure a struggle with any disease and come out with pure golden health in the end. You need to realize that God can use an apparently worthless illness to build more faith in us, cause us to seek Him more, and to allow us to become sensitive to the pain others feel while enduring a sickness in their own bodies.

God allowed His servant Job to be afflicted with boils all over his body and allowed all of Job's sons and daughters to be killed so that Job's only dependence and trust would be in God and not in anything else. God will remove even good things from our lives if they begin to distract us from a passionate relationship with Him. God is very jealous concerning us! Now to human sight, this seems like an unnecessary waste of good material. However, God never wishes for us to give more attention to things or people within our lives than we give to Him. Therefore, He simply breathes on them and causes them to either dry up or die.

I hope that you are really beginning to understand how worthless things can truly become useful in the hand of a very creative and powerful God. Here is another scenario. God may require you to sow your entire mortgage for your home payment into someone else's life for the payment of his or her mortgage. If this should happen to you, first make sure that it is God by seeking another confirming dream, spoken word, prophecy, or spiritual sign. Once you know that this is God, you may wonder why God would tell you to forgo payment of your mortgage in order to pay off that of another believer. You may wonder why God would not tell you to give that money to a great preacher or even to your pastor. Well, here are some possible reasons as to why God would ask such a foolish, worthless thing of you. It might be that God knows that you have never been late with your house payments and, therefore, you would not be at risk for losing your house because of one late payment. However, the believer that you are being asked to give your mortgage money to, will lose her house if she does not pay her mortgage right away. Also, God is trying to give you a better house from this sacrificial seed that He is asking you to sow—a house that you have always been asking Him to release to you in a debt-free manner. However, if you decide that what God is requiring of you is much too stupid, worthless, and crazy, and you do not obey Him, then you would end up cursing your blessing and possibly one day losing even the house which you currently possess.

We must be careful in these present times of struggle to do all that God requires of us. We do not know what worthless things He is allowing into our lives that will be of the greatest use in bringing us closer to Him or closer to our destiny and blessing. Therefore, before we throw away or dismiss anything or anyone as being worthless or useless, we had better place it under a serious God-check. This means that we must allow God's Spirit and His word to perform the examination for us and then speak to us the true and real diagnosis.

Once you have witnessed some of the worthless things which God has used and made very useful, you may want to know how God does it. Yes, indeed! How does God cause the most dead and decaying things to give birth to the most alive and creative things? Furthermore, how does God make cursed things cause great blessings to flow? What is even more confusing is how God can make great things out of nothing? Well, if you are as inquisitive as I am, then you would definitely want to know the answers to these mind-stalling questions. Does it not hurt your brain, trying to wrap your mind around such deep questions? I know it hurts mine! However, what helps me to be comforted and to sleep far better at night is knowing that I will never know the answers to many questions, but I know the God who does! Therefore, let us allow God, by His Holy Spirit, the chance to answer these questions for us.

The first truth you should know concerning how God is able to make dead things birth living things, make cursed things yield great blessings, and make great things out of nothing at all is simply because He is God. You see, as God, He has all conceivable power and authority. His nature of being all-powerful allows Him to not only make anything, but to make it in His own way and to fit it into His plans. God can bend time to fit His purpose. He can bend death to make it do what it normally cannot do, that is, to make life. God has enough miraculous power to cause anything to exist, without anything physically around to birth it or conceive it. God is a living womb, filled with every life within Himself, and thus is able to create all life by Himself. He is just God!

The second answer to such important questions is that God has living words. Every word spoken by God is charged with the potential to cause life or take life. Every word echoed from the mountain of God's dominion can either create or destroy. When God speaks, His words are able to cause great changes in eternity or time, heaven or earth, which can last for one day or even for an eternity. God always speaks words which will change the very nature of things. For example, in the Bible, scripture references how God spoke and out of nothing came all life. He changed the nature of nothing and made it become more than it was capable of becoming. Then, there are references to God causing barren wombs to give birth. God was able to cause infertile women to give birth to many children. In addition, He was able to close the wombs of some women until it was the right God-moment for them to conceive the right child from God. Oh, yes, God's very words are a living womb of creation!

A third answer for how God is able to do the aforementioned things is by His ever-living and ever-present Spirit. The Spirit of God is also His divine breath, which enables God to be everywhere at once and capable of producing life anywhere. The Holy Spirit carries God's power and creative force where it is much needed and creates the most awesome things just by His divine breath. Do you recall how God formed Adam out of dust? Then, instead of using His word life, God decided to use His breath life, the Holy Ghost, to breathe life into that which was dead. God made a living spirit and soul being out of His creative and living Holy Spirit breath. In the church of Jesus Christ today, the Holy Spirit is active, giving chosen men and women enough power from God's breath to preach people into heaven, deliver them from diseases, prophesy things yet to come, and to know great mysteries by the revelatory power of God. As a matter of fact, many miraculous signs and wonders are being done every day. God is very much alive and at work among us, creating life and causing worthless things to change their nature and become very necessary and useful. Let us be thankful that we have a God who can do all this!

I wish to reiterate to you to check that which appears worthless in your life before you get rid of it. You must be very careful not to damage your own spiritual growth and blessing by throwing out useful things that come in the worthless-looking package. I believe that God sends us the most useful things but wraps them in ugly, worthless boxes to see if we are paying attention to the ways in which He moves. Be careful not to curse the gift simply because it is not packaged or wrapped to your liking!

RECYCLE
it, Baby

All of the pain inflicted upon your life is to be recycled to deliver others who are in present pain!

In this life, whether we are a born-again Christian or a sinner, we will all go through moments of great pain. Hurts, bumps, and bruises are a part of life's journey. However, as easy as it is for me to admit that pain is definitely a part of everyday life, it is more difficult to have to experience that pain. You might be one of the many billions of people on this planet that has had your share of painful events and experiences. For those newly saved, you probably would like to quickly forget all the pain which has occurred in your past now that you are a newly born child of God; please do not do this. Now I know that suggesting such a thing is like revisiting your pain, but you must realize that all the negative events and the pain of your past are to be recycled and used by God as a testimony to others who cannot believe that they will ever make it through their pain. Oh, yes, indeed! Your past pain and your present peace are both powerful tools of witness which reveal that God is able to help people endure their present pain and then deliver them from it. Therefore, the memories which seem so horrific to you due to the many hardships from your past must be recycled and used to help bring the peace of God into the nightmarish reality of so many others.

God who is the chief collector of dust (worthless things) is able to harness all the memories of the painful experiences of our past and reuse them to birth hope within the countless numbers of people who have no real hope in this life. Therefore, our pain is another person's healing! Our torment becomes another person's peace! And our weak moments become another person's strength! Please do not throw away the memories of your pain. Recycle them, and allow God to bring comfort and deliverance to many lives on this earth. You owe this much to every broken soul, seeing that Jesus gave Himself over to pain, agony, and terrible trauma so that we would be able to escape the far greater pain and agony of hell. Think about that! Jesus Christ, the awesome God in human flesh, took on Himself all our afflictions, sins, diseases, and pains. Each one of His scars represents the scars of our sinful and judged lives. Each one of His scars represent how abused and messed up our earthly lives were. Although His life in heaven was without wounds, He ventured down to earth to take on Himself a life filled with bruises, so that we might experience His peace. Now if Jesus Christ did all this, then surely we could allow our scars to be seen by others. When we are not afraid to reveal our scars to others, then they will be able to see that our awesome God is able to heal all their scars. In the same manner that Jesus was not afraid to reveal His scars to His disciple, Thomas, we too should not hide our scars. Although our scars might be ugly, they represent badges of honor unto the God who has healed all of our past hurts and wounds. Therefore, see God's beauty within your scars and let them reveal how God can completely heal every weak and wounded life.

You and I have got to get to the place in our spiritual maturity where we will no longer hide the scars of a painful life. We must realize that Satan wants us to hide those scars because he knows they would be an awesome witness of God's healing touch. Therefore, the worst thing that we can do with the memories of the scars of our past is to hide them away in the deep closets of our minds where no one can see them and be touched by the God-designed beauty within them.

Since you now know this truth, do not ever hide your scars as if you are ashamed of your past. Remember that if you have scars, this probably means that your wounds were healed. If you were healed, this probably means that God's healing touch had everything to do with your now-healed life. Please do not hide those beautiful scars. Recycle them and use them! For example, if you are a single Christian who has been wounded by the loss of your virginity, do not live in shame because of it. If you have already confessed this to God and He has healed you, your life can be a witness to other young single persons. Let them see how that mistake in your life did not kill your God-birthed purpose. Allow them to see that God can take their lives and make them His true children, not just another man's or woman's play toy. Oh yeah, baby! Recycle and use all the pain of being used to be a warning sign to other young singles on how to avoid being played in a sexual game by no-good pimps and hustlers. Your painful past that you think is so ugly might just be the witness of the Lord's beauty to someone else who is experiencing ugliness in their lives.

Now, maybe you have had an abortion in your past and, after accepting Jesus Christ and being made new, you have just discovered that due to excessive scarring from that operation, you will not be able to have any children. You feel devastated and you just want to lie down in a bed of guilt and depression and die. Although you might feel all torn up inside, I wish to give you this good news. God still has plans for your life and, most important, He has plans for this scar. With this in mind, you need to get up and get into worship. You now have an opportunity to recycle this bad memory into something far better. You can use this as a witness to other young women concerning the dangers of abortion, as well as to offer hope of God's salvation and healing for those who have had an abortion. Your pain is waiting to be their healing. And your agony is waiting for the chance to be their peace. In fact, your past defeat will turn into another person's present victory. Please share and testify how God has delivered you from the guilt and wound of this horrible experience. Let the world know that God has taken you out of the dust of being a killer of life and has given you His image to now help preserve life. You are now beautiful! God made you beautiful! And your scar is very beautiful!

If you have been, or currently are, in prison due to a badly wounded life of crime and now are walking with God, do not be discouraged or ashamed of this scar. I realize that some people might never forgive you because of what you have done in your past. I also realize that some will forever look at your present life and remember the wounds of your past. However, you must see yourself through the eyes of God and not the poor, judgmental vision of other people. There are many people who are waiting to hear the story of your once broken but now mended life. Many of them are in jail with you and are waiting for you to share with them the God who transformed your wounds into healed scars. For those who are now out of prison, you have the opportunity to use your scars as a warning to others. Let them know that they do not have to slip and fall into a life of crime. Show them the full length of your scar, with the hope that this will terrify them enough to keep them from that path and maybe even inspire them to allow God to change them if they have already begun a life of crime.

God also wants you to take that painful memory of a bad divorce, reveal the scar that you now have, and show other Christians that life does not end at divorce but can really begin anew by God's awesome power. I realize that once you are divorced, many closed-minded and judgmental Christians believe that God can never use you. In fact, some of them do not even consider that it might have been your spouse and not you who cheated and broke the marital covenant. However, even if you were the cause of this divorce, if you have made your peace with God and have received a full pardon from Him, you can use this scar as an example of how God can deliver us from our greatest mistakes. Do not live in fear of your ugly scar! You might be thinking to yourself, *What can my divorce offer to anyone?* Well, I believe that the answer is that of a very important life lesson. Oh yes, the mistake or the mistakes made in this divorce experience might just be a sign and visible life lesson to those who think of marriage as just some game or to those who are attempting to rush into marriage. You can be used by God to help married couples be true to their mates and never take them for granted, through the testimony of the mistakes made by either you or your ex-spouse. Therefore, do not be silent. Let your scar speak!

There are some of you Christians out there that might be hiding the fact that you never finished high school. Yes, it is true that you have a good job and that you take care of your family very well. However, you have been carrying around this hidden shame for years. In fact, you have carried this shame like a heavy weight around your neck for so long that you are just about to collapse under the strain of this failure. I wish for you to be encouraged! This is not the end of the world, and in Christ you are worth more than a high school diploma. Find a night school and get an equivalent document to a high school diploma. It's not too late! You also need to stop hiding this scar from your family. Harness the raw potential of this scar and use it to warn your children of the dangers of not finishing high school. Recycle and use this ugly experience by speaking to young people in the church concerning the importance of staying in school. Share with them that if they have been goofing off in the classroom, there is still time for them to turn things around and become serious, just like you have by going back to get your GED. This scar in your life reveals how God, by His awesome power, could provide for an entire family through a father or mother who has never even finished high school. Therefore, this scar represents a beautiful miracle from God!

In another reality, there might be some of you who are Christians and are struggling with AIDS. Maybe you contracted this terrible disease while you were living a very loose and godless life, but now you are passionate about God and the things of God. I believe that you are not only in physical pain, but you are also in emotional pain. You are in emotional pain because you know that over the years, the Church has not really dealt with people with AIDS in a very loving manner, and you are scared that if some in your local church fellowship were to find out that you have AIDS, they might shun you and no longer want to fellowship with you. I want to inform you that in Jesus Christ, you are not an AIDS victim. You are more than a conqueror! You are a child of the King over all kings! You are not a disgrace, but you have been saved by grace! You are the most important thing to God in this life! Now that you know these things, you do not need to be ashamed anymore. This ugly scar in your life is a beautiful representation of the kindness of God. It reveals how God can save us from the most dirty and dusty lifestyle. Your scar also shows that God loves us right in the mud of our sinful lives and is not afraid to reach down, get His hands dirty, and lift us out of this muddy experience. God wants you to testify to His people, by the power of His Holy Spirit, about the dangers of walking down a lustful and non-marital sexual path. Then, reveal to other Christians who also have this dreadful disease that their lives are not over. The same God who can heal them from the mental wound of this disease can heal them from the physical manifestation of this disease as well. So, go ahead. Let them see your scar!

I believe that at this time, and by all that the Holy Spirit has revealed to us about recycling our worst memories, we should all be more comfortable in showing off our scars. We must be mindful that our scars are more for other people than they are for us. Our recycled scars serve as evidence of the awesome healing power of God. God is able to use them to help others avoid making very drastic mistakes and to provide them with hope that there is deliverance from every pit of every mistake. Therefore, we must not ever be afraid to remember our wounds. We must not ever be afraid to remember our pains and hurts. And, we must never ever hide any scar in our lives because it stands as a great testimony of the existence, power, and love of our one true living God!

The memories of your broken, painful, bruised, battered, abused, and raped past must not be wasted by being thrown away, but recycled as a witness that the God who brought you out alive is the same God who can bring out alive those who are where you once were!

6

Only those who are NOT afraid to BECOME dust carry God's Breath

---

It is only when we allow ourselves to be reduced to nothing in God's hands that we can be made into something worth carrying God's breath!

One day Rock and Dust came before God to ask that He use them in the service of His powerful purpose. God looked at Rock and asked that he tell Him the reasons why He should choose to use him for His purpose. After Rock had some time to think about God's question, he then proceeded to share all of his fascinating accolades, which he believed would cause God to choose him over Dust. Rock talked about how he was strong, sturdy, and dependable. He further boasted that he would never be moved, no matter the pressure. After hearing this, God told Rock that these were very good qualities. Then God turned to Dust and asked that he tell Him why he would be a better candidate than Rock for His purpose. Dust began to think about the question and came up with only one answer. The answer that Dust gave to God was not that he was strong, sturdy, or dependable. However, Dust told God that he would simply be willing to be made into anything God would wish in order to do whatever God would require of him. Now Rock, believing that he would be the clear and sure choice, began to gloat and push up his chest. God turned to them both and informed them which one He would choose. He looked directly into the face of Rock and told him that although he was strong, sturdy, and dependable, he would not be chosen. When Rock inquired of God why it was that He had chosen Dust over him, God gave him this answer: he was already all that he could ever be; however, Dust could still be made into anything which God desired. The simple, but wonderful, moral of this story is that when we come to God already made up or dressed up in the way we think would make Him want to use us, He cannot use us. God wants to take people who are unmade and then make them over. Those who will not humble themselves and ask God to transform them into the vessel of His choice will never be the vessel that He chooses.

If we were to approach God like Rock did, we would be turned away. God would have no use for us, seeing that we would not allow Him to give us His shape and form and thinking that our own egos, skills, and gifts would make us suitable enough for God to use. Now, don't you think that this is quite arrogant and presumptuous of us? I would think so indeed! Therefore, if you and I are going to be suitable for the work and will of God, we must become like dust in His hands. In fact, we are going to have to put aside what we think we should be for God, and allow Him the opportunity to make us what He wishes.

There is a biblical story that illustrates how we must become like dust in order to be used by God. This story relates how God told one of His Old Testament prophets to go down to the potter's house and observe him at work. When the prophet arrived at the house of the pot maker, he noticed that as the potter worked with a piece of clay, forming it into a definite shape, the vessel cracked. The potter had to rework the clay and make it into another vessel. This awesome illustration reveals that the clay does not tell the potter what to make it into; the potter decides what type of vessel would best suit the clay and his needs. Another lesson that we can glean from this beautiful illustration is that the clay was a kind of material that was easily fashioned, molded, and shaped into practically any design of the potter's choosing. We need to be like this piece of clay. We should put aside our own will and allow God to shape and mold us His way. After all, He created us and He is the only Being who knows the complete blueprint of what we are best suited to be made into and how we are best suited to be used.

We should know by now that those who want to be their own maker will never experience God's awesome power actively at work in their lives. As seen in the book of Genesis, God only breathes His most pure life into dead, dust-like vessels. God does this so that all the praise and honor of what is made will only go to Him and not to the vessel itself. Just as brilliant painters or sculptors place their signature on their work of art so people will know that it was they alone who created such a masterpiece, God does the same. At the end of the day, God wants others to come to know Him as the architect, artist, and sculptor who can take their ugly, out-of-form life and make it into a spiritual work of art.

We must realize that God alone sees the blueprint concerning all that we are meant to become. God is the master Creator of all life, and all life receives its purpose and exact design from God. Thus, if any life is to be born or created, it will become so by the word and Spirit of God. Also, if any life is to have relevance in this world, it is going to have to receive that relevance from God. We are not living beings by chance. We all have been designed, and the reasons for such a design are completely in the capable mind of God. Therefore, the only way to learn of His wonderful design would be to submit ourselves to the creative power and presence of God. We must realize that without God we are nothing, and to become whatever it is that God wishes will require and demand that we become like dust. You and I must let God touch us in whatever way He likes because only God knows how to touch our dust form and make it become heaven's form. Long before we were born, we had already existed in the creative mind of God. Therefore, all that we are supposed to do and become is hidden in God, just waiting to be discovered by us.

Another reason we must be reduced to dust in order to carry God's breath is that God will never breathe the fullness of Himself into any vessel that will not allow Him to rule. A rebellious people cannot carry the full breath of God's ever-present Spirit within their lives because the breath of God does not allow continuous rebellion; it consumes it. If the breath of God were to live within a person who spurns the very rules of God's kingdom, this individual would soon be torn apart by the hurricane-like strength of God's Spirit breath. However, when we become dust and allow God to lead us or blow us in whatever direction that His holy will desires, then we are able to carry His awesome breath of healing, miracles, and spiritual gifts into a world that is out of breath. Thus, in order to carry God's breath with us and within us, we must allow the Holy Spirit to tell us where to go, what to be, and how to live. We must never attempt to dictate to God where we wish to evangelize, to whom we wish to preach, or to whom we prefer to help. We must remember that if God is going to breathe His power into us, then we are going to have to commit our entire being in obedience to God's breath.

You see, God's greatness can only be revealed through our smallness. We see this in John the Baptist's example. When Jesus Christ showed up in human form to bring to the dying world the most awesome move of God, John the Baptist told the people that he had to now decrease so that Jesus could increase. Then, let us not forget how God told a man called Gideon to reduce an army of more than ten thousand to three hundred so that they would experience victory. You see, the smaller we become through testing and weakness, the more power and greatness of our God will be seen. It is only when we are allowed by God to be sick and then allow Him, not the doctors, to miraculously heal us that people will realize the true depths of God's power. God constantly wants us to be weak so that close friends and family members around us will see that it was never our own strength keeping us alive. Listen, God is willing to allow houses to be taken from us, spouses to divorce us, and jobs to be withheld from us so that He can step in and rescue us. He does this to prove to every one who watched us be stripped, and laughed at our stripping, that human strength will always fail, but His power lasts forever. Think about it! God allowed His Son to be humiliated, stripped, and treated as if He were not of God nor from God so that He could reveal His awesome power to us through the weakness of Jesus Christ. Therefore, when we consider that Jesus did not shy away from becoming like dust in order to expose us to an all-powerful God, then we should not be angry with God for bringing us down into some dusty pits in order to reveal Himself to others that need to see Him.

Would you still like to know more about why God would allow us to be reduced to nothing but dust so that we can carry His breath? God's breath is so precious to Him, that in order for any vessel to carry such a creative and living breath, they have to be able to go anywhere and everywhere on God's behalf. Take a look at physical dust. Dust can be found just about anywhere and everywhere. If you go into the ghetto, you will find it. Should you go into very wealthy neighborhoods, you will find it there as well. In the borders of your own country, you will find dust. And if you were to visit a foreign country, dust would be there as well. There is truly no escaping the reality that dust is everywhere. Since God wants His breath to be everywhere, He is always in need of people who are not afraid to take His breath to rich houses or poor houses, gang territories or peaceful communities, and upscale neighborhoods or poverty-stricken ghettos. God wants people of all cultures, colors, religions, and nationalities to inhale His breath of salvation. Therefore, any person who would shy away from this challenge is not going to carry God's breath and will not be able to truly change this world. As physical dust is obviously not afraid to be found anywhere, all those who aspire to be filled with the power of the Holy Ghost and the fullness of God's breath must also not be afraid.

As we continue this study of why people must be reduced to dust to carry God's breath, we will discover that another reason which supports this principle is that heaven works best when earth stops trying. The moment in which you and I stop trying to save ourselves, stop relying solely on doctors for healing, and stop depending on people or human connections to bail us out of our problems is the moment that God can breathe His life-changing breath into our dead and decaying circumstances. We need to stop trying to make situations work out, and let God influence the very atmosphere itself. It is encouraging to know that God does not merely deliver us through life's storms; He can change the very nature of the storm. If we stop trying to use our human intellect to worm or wiggle our way out of every disaster within our lives, then God will give us just the right of amount of His breath and turn our so-called disasters into mere toys for our amusement. Please be aware that until we take our breath out of the equation, God will never breathe His into our situations.

Now, once you and I have allowed ourselves to be reduced to the likeness of mere dust, we can become so filled with God's breath that we truly witness the power of our living God. Who among us would wish to throw away the opportunity to carry the most miraculous, life-creating breath that will ever be? I would hope that none of us would! We must open our eyes and see that when we carry the breath of God, many things can happen. First of all, the breath of God makes dead things spring to life. The presence of God's breath saves the sinner's condemned soul by giving them a new and living spirit. When we allow room for the breath of God, His powerful blowing Spirit, then family members for whom we have been praying for years will be saved. Not only will salvation take place, but also the healing of sick bodies. When the breath of God enters a disease-stricken body, it begins to kill the very disease that was causing the body to die. In fact, there is no disease alive within the human body that can withstand the power of one lone breath from God. When God exhales, sickness becomes deflated.

When permitted, the breath of God is also able to provide prophetic and supernatural insight or vision concerning events in your past, present, and future. When we accept that a dust position is not our end position, God will transfer enough of His breath to us and will show us happenings in our family's past, events in our personal present, and very important situations in our future. Think about this! You and I will be able to realize how sins and wicked influences came to be within our family and how they are presently affecting us. We will also recognize satanic traps right around us and avoid them. Then, we could be comforted by the truth that God has some major futuristic plans for us.

When we flow in God's breath, He releases His wisdom to provide us with answers for very pressing and serious problems. We will know how to walk correctly and act almost perfectly in every situation. This wisdom from God would help us to open businesses and keep our homes in correct kingdom order. This is just another wonderful result of having God's breath within us.

God's breath does even more cool stuff. For example, His breath in our lives would give us the ability to experience miracles. Oh, yes! Wherever the breath of God appears, miracles are always possible. God can use us to raise the dead, literally! He can open blind eyes through us. By the laying on of hands, God can cause cancer cells to dry up and die. With the miraculous presence of the breath of God, we can cause the wealth of nations to be attracted to us. If you allow God to breathe on your debt by sowing a life of righteousness and sowing financial seeds of your earnings, then the power of God will so breathe onto your bank account or your stocks that your net worth could literally double.

Well, now you know what an incredible experience it would be to walk through this life with the breath of God. I would rather have one breath from God than one thousand breaths of human connection and intelligence. This is because anything birthed from human beings will eventually fail. Therefore, if I am in an airplane, I would want God's breath rather than any kind of flotation device. The same is true in this life. Give me God's breath, and you can keep the flotation devices of money, power, human networks, and fame. When all of these run out of breath, I will still be inhaling more of God's breath.

You should also know the serious dangers involved with being without God's breath. When we are without or have ran out of God's breath due to a faithless and sinful life, then we are exposed to the failing breath of human weakness. In other words, when the breath of God is absent, we tend to solely rely on family, friends, jobs, and money. We seek fulfillment in these things, but we usually end up more alone and hurt because of them. If God's breath is absent, human breath is all that is left, and this is never enough! It is a sad condition to live for this life alone and have no reserved breath for the life to come.

Life without God's breath does not afford one the ability to fight against the demonic kingdom of Satan and the fallen race of angels. There is no victory against their lies, strategies, and distractions. Without the breath of God, we would simply be at the mercy of these supernatural beings. Therefore, it is a dangerous position to be marked and called by God and then not full of His breath. Many Christians who have attempted to wage war against such demonic foes, without the breath of God, have been totally annihilated! We must not be like them!

Now, you should know that when I write about the breath of God, I am referring to His manifested Holy Spirit. Since God is a very diverse Being, it is safe to see Him as Father (Divine Design Thinker), Word (Divine Manifested Function), and Holy Spirit (Divine Breath Operation). God is able to think great thoughts, manifest them through His word, and make them alive in order to operate by His Holy Spirit. Yet, He is one God—not many. What a deep and mysterious God! Since God allows His Spirit to cause everything which He has designed to operate, then all living and functioning things have, at one time or another, been influenced by His breath. Therefore, we who are now born again or born of the Spirit have been greatly influenced by God's breath. In the same way that hurricanes are of differing categories based on their wind velocity, so too are there different levels of our experience with the breath of God. The first level of our experience with God's breath is the new birth. This occurs after we have heard the

Gospel of Jesus Christ. The Holy Spirit begins to court our dead spirit and condemned soul until we give into this courtship and accept the invitation of salvation and future supper of the bridegroom, Jesus Christ. Now, this level of God's breath is good in that it delivers us from hell and makes us one with God; however, demons are not moved just because we are now saved.

In order to handle greater battles on the horizon, we have to receive the next level of God's breath, which is the baptism of the Holy Ghost. When this occurs, God gives us massively bold strength. Then He turns on or activates the weapons of the Holy Spirit, which give us His divine protective power against demons. Finally, He unleashes His many gifts of the Holy Spirit. With these gifts, we are able to help edify or strengthen other Christians in their struggle with the demonic realm. Therefore, the second level of the breath of God gives us power over every satanic temptation or trap. Any Christian lacking the second level hurricane wind of the breath of God will never last in the face of this satanic warfare. Our ability to inhale God's breath represents the reality that we have been made children of God. However, we must be able to exhale God's breath upon others, which is this second level of the experience with His breath. It is here that we can cast out demons, heal the sick, discern demonic spirits, prophesy future events, know present situations, and walk heavily armed with the weapons that are the very character of God Himself, such as truth, righteousness, the Gospel of peace, faith, salvation, and the Word of God. Please understand that with these weapons of God's character upon us, we will be able to discern every lie and never live a life of lies. We would be able to beat sin and the temptation to sin because of the right to live righteous. With the Gospel of peace, we would never be drowned by the fear of our storms. By using the weapon of faith, mountains would not even exist to us. Also, as we deploy the weapon of salvation, we would never live in fear of the wrath of God; this would be strength in and of itself. Once we utilized the Word of God, we would be able to have possibilities where before there was only impossibilities. We would be so built up in faith, heaven would open up every window and door over our lives.

After all that the Holy Spirit has shared thus far concerning God's breath, I hope you see that we cannot live without the abiding presence of the Holy Spirit. Therefore, we should not fear becoming like dust since it would mean that the Holy Spirit would continue to live in us and work through us. Isn't this the highest form of life? There is no life, nor way of life, higher than being born of and filled with the Holy Spirit. He is the divine breath of God.

MOVING FROM
DUST *form*
TO *Spirit* FORM

---

*Never be willing to remain in a place where
your destiny was not designed to live!*

I want you to be encouraged and know that you do not have to live based upon how and where you were born. Although you received a dust birth from sinful Adam, you are now in Jesus Christ and, as a result, have been granted access into a better birth and a greater destiny. Even though you and I were born dead to the things of God and alive to the world of sin and decay, we do not have to live under the power of this death. Jesus has lifted us out of the dirt of alcoholism, poverty, ungodly sexual pleasures, twisted passions, and every evil thing designed by Satan to send us to an early grave and to a

Christ-less hell. This is reason for celebration! Yes, you might have begun your life in poverty, but you do not have to be buried there. Yes, you might have inherited a bad drinking habit from your father or mother, but you do not have to drink yourself into an early grave. Yes, you might have been raped or sexually molested when you were a young child, but you do not have to live in the shadow of this memory as a victim. Oh, yes, Jesus Christ has now given you a destiny far greater, more wonderful, and completely purified from all this dirt of your past. You are more beautiful than the ugliness that has plagued your past. You are of greater value than how you were treated in your former life because of the blood of Jesus Christ. Take great pleasure in knowing that the Holy Spirit wants to take you from a dust form and transport you into a spirit form.

What I mean by the term spirit form is the complete growth and development of the new inner you, which just happens to be God's new DNA released to you. Therefore, becoming spirit form means to act and live according to the same qualities found in the life of Jesus Christ, as revealed in the biblical Gospels and taught by the first-century apostles in the New Testament letters. If you are a child of God, then you have been given His very life, and this life can be seen through acts which display God's real and visible nature. So, although people cannot physically see God's face, they will be able to see God's nature, as revealed through you.

In order for you to move from a life of meaningless dust into one of meaningful spirit form, you must first come to the place of realization. I wish, by the revelation of the Holy Spirit, to call this the Principle of Realization. Think about it. No one is able to change until he or she comes to the realization that change is needed. So many Christians, even though they have entered God's kingdom, still remain unchanged by His power because they simply refuse to realize that they need to change. When we refuse to realize that we need to grow, change, and leave some things behind, then we are destined to remain in the dusty grave of staying as we are. It is very difficult for us to admit (come into the realization) that we are wrong or that we have much more spirit development to undergo. As human beings, we do not like to be wrong or for others to tell us we are wrong. We often get offended at others telling us that we might have spoken the wrong word or that we might have made a very costly mistake. You see, we believe that being wrong somehow lessens our value or our ability to bring any worthwhile and lasting contribution to this world. Therefore, we tend to hide from our wrong and enter a state of denial, so we don't have to deal with any wrong that we might have done. There is real danger in this! If we are truly wrong or have sinned and refused to realize it, then we would not be able to confess it unto God. Thus, God will not be able to cleanse us from it. If we are not cleansed from the stigma of sin because of denial, then we are doomed to live under the filthy dirty power of that sin. This will hinder our move from a weakened dust form into a powerful spirit form. Now, I know that you do not want to live as if sickness is greater than you or as if this world's addictions are too strong for you to break. I would think not! Therefore, when you make a mistake, do not be afraid to realize it, own it, and then confess it. This is the path to your cleansing and spiritual transformation.

A second requirement for you to move from dust form into spirit form would be the Principle of Release. It is a very common and factual principle that in order to catch a second fish on one line, you must first release the first fish you caught. Therefore, in order to take up the far more superior life of spirit, you must be willing to live a life of letting go of, or releasing, dusty flesh. In essence, if you want to always speak truthfully, you must start by releasing lies from your tongue. If you wish to be faithful to your wife, you should not have your mind tied to another woman. If you wish to follow hard after God, you must release anything that is a dangerous distraction in your life. Jesus told us in the New Testament that we cannot serve two masters at the same time. This is a very true principle. So many Christians have never really lived to the full potential of the life of God within their living spirits because they have decided that the pleasures and lusts of this present world are worth more to them. Some of them are still attempting to hold onto God, while clenching every ungodly thing in the palm of their hands. Well, this will not work.

Let us consider this from another perspective. What if you had slipped off a cliff, and the only thing that kept you from falling was a skinny little branch. Now, this branch is not going to hold your body weight for very long, and you are starting to panic. All of a sudden, you look up at the ledge and see a hand reaching down to you. You hear the voice of a rescuer telling you to let go and grab onto his hand. Even though you have help, if you do not release the branch and grasp the hand of your rescuer, you will probably soon fall to your death. So, you see, in order to be saved, you have to release that which can only hold you for so long. This illustration reveals how many Christians are missing out on the fullness of the Lord's Spirit by refusing to let go of their past sinful, dusty lives. God wants to deliver them from alcoholism, but they refuse to let go of the very bottle of liquor that is killing them. Then there are those who are so busy looking for love in the form of sexual promiscuity that they cannot even see that God has already brought their Mr. or Miss Right to them. There are also many whom God wants to take out of poverty, but they refuse to sow financial seeds into His Church; therefore, they continue to live in a poverty which God never chose for them.

A farmer understands that in order for the land to yield a new harvest for him, he has to release the necessary seed. Therefore, he quickly releases seed in the season of sowing, knowing full well that the soil will protect the seed and will make a harvest that could feed his entire family for a long time. However, if he holds onto the seeds tightly and does not release them, then neither the ground nor the seeds will benefit him, and he will starve. Whatever you must let go of in your life in order to enter the harvest of spirit form, please let it go. There is a greater form for your life, but you must first release all the negative and lesser forms produced by sin and rebellion. And, remember: no matter what you release, you can trust that God will grant unto you a far better life, form, and harvest. There is no doubt in my mind. I believe that God is waiting for you to let go of sinful, troublesome friends and any evil distractions in your life so that He can take you to places in His Spirit you can't even imagine. Let it go, baby! Let it go!

The next way you can move from dust form into spirit form is by practicing the Principle of Discipline. Discipline is the state of training and conditioning which allows the weakest believer to become a spiritually strong believer. When God called us in Jesus Christ, He called us to walk in a lifestyle of great discipline. The life of discipline into which we must walk is one of pursuing godliness. We must be in a constant state of living in truth, practicing love, seeking God's truth in the study of His Word, and spending great moments having intimate connections with Him in private prayer. We must allow ourselves the time to think pure thoughts, by conditioning our minds to listen to sermons, spiritual songs, and positive words. The more that we are able to exercise this kind of discipline over our minds, the more we will bring our mortal bodies under God's great control. Once we continue to live disciplined lives by renewing our thoughts, guarding what enters our minds and bodies, and giving ourselves over to time spent in prayer and fasting, then we will truly be setting up our lives to become Spirit-formed.

We must also remember that God wants us to live very disciplined lives. In fact, God is a very disciplined Being. He never allows even one word that He speaks to remain unfulfilled. When there is no discipline, we tend to get caught up in the wrong things and be in the wrong places at the wrong times. It is only when we are mentally, physically, and spiritually disciplined that we can live on a far higher plane of spiritual existence. Then and only then will the power of God's nature be able to move and flow through us. Therefore, no discipline equals no spiritual maturity. No spiritual maturity equals no real walk with God! And, no real walk with God would leave us spiritually deformed and stunted. This would make us very easy prey for Satan to mislead, mistreat, mishandle, and defeat. Any believer who will not walk in a very disciplined way will soon get lost among the crowd of sinners who will do and say anything in this present world. Thus, discipline is one of the narrow paths leading to a spirit-formed life.

As we move further along in our understanding of what it takes to move from dust form into spirit form, we must be prepared to live according to the Hunger Principle. This principle represents a passionate desire or drive for something of great and valuable importance. No one on this planet will ever possess or earn anything of great worth unless he or she is willing to passionately pursue it, driven by a great hunger. As a matter of fact, Jesus Christ preached from the pages of the New Testament that only those who develop a hunger and thirst for all that is righteous would ever be filled. Therefore, if we are going to walk in the character of God we must have an intense longing for the character of God. Please consider that when we are not physically hungry, we do not want to eat. Spiritually, we are the same way. Additionally, wherever there is great hunger for living life in accordance to the Spirit of God, God's goodness and righteousness will be at work. You and I can never move from a life of selfish pride, ungodly lust, and wicked thoughts until we develop a hunger for the pure things of God's Spirit. You see, if I wish to change the bad behavior in my life, I must first have a hunger for the good behavior of God. Then and only then will I have the aid of God's Spirit and the power of His righteousness to help me change. I am amazed at how many people confess Jesus Christ as Lord and Savior but never allow His nature to truly change their sinful one. Just because we believe that God is real does not mean that we have accepted Him as our God. Also, just because we have received Him into our lives as our Savior does not necessarily mean that we will live according to His character. Only those who have a strong hunger to be changed from a life of dust into one of spirit will ever experience such a beautiful change. Think about this! When we get tired of being abused by sin or battered and confused by sin, we will begin to realize that there is a far better life for us. When we begin to long for that far better life found only in constant fellowship with Jesus, then God will replace our empty lives with a spirit-filled one. Therefore, if we are going to move from dust form into spirit form, then the Hunger Principle must be unleashed!

Another way we will become spirit formed and escape the sinful existence of our old dust form is by applying the Mimic Principle. The word mimic means to see something and imitate it. Since God is a spirit and has no physical body as His natural makeup then we must mimic His ways if we are going to become a spirit form like Him. We cannot truly shake off the limitations of our frail human dust form until we put on the essence or quality of God's Spirit form. And, the only way we can put on the beautiful quality of a spirit-formed life is by living in a spirit-formed manner. God, just like any good parent, wishes for all of His children to walk in His shoes. Thus, in order for this to be possible, God literally placed His spiritual DNA or spiritual genetic code in each of us. Therefore, since God is love, we who are His children should walk in love. Also, God is filled with joy and creates everything out of this wonderful character. So, all God's children should be filled with joy, no matter how much of life's bitterness is thrown our way.

In addition, we must strive to walk in peace since God is always at peace even in the midst of life's symbolic storms. God is so much at peace that when Jesus was on the ship in the middle of a storm, He was sleeping. This is how we ought to act. When they come to repossess your house, just walk in the peace of God. Since God never panics, you do not have to panic! Look into the face of your storm, get into worship, and know that the peace of God is your very peace! Furthermore, in order to become spirit form by mimicking God, we have to walk in longsuffering. Longsuffering is the spiritual ability to stay long in any storm, to outlast even the strength of a storm.

God can love us beyond our many years of ignoring Him because He can outlast our own stubbornness. When the child of God walks like this, he or she can endure anything and make it through everything. God is also very gentle. Therefore, if we are going to be spirit formed, we are going to have to mimic God and handle abrasive people and situations with a gentle nature.

Another characteristic of God is that He is filled with goodness. He can do no evil. Since He put this same quality within us, we must be good in the midst of an increasingly wicked world. We can do this, and we will be spirit formed every time we walk in goodness. God is a God of pure faith. He can never doubt; therefore, every word that He speaks will never fail. Can you believe that we have this same ability hidden away within us? Well, we do! We have the ability to speak in such faith that we can move mountains, or even create them! God is very meek! God's meekness was seen when He allowed His son, Jesus Christ, to be slaughtered so our lives could be spared. In essence, God punished His son for sins for which we should have died. Now, this is awesome! We have to be as meek as our God. This cruel world, filled with some people who attempt to harm us, needs for us to approach them with great meekness. And by the power of God's character, we can! Finally, God is very temperate, which means that He is always in complete control of Himself. Those of us who are His children must be self-controlled as well. We must guard what our eyes see, what our ears hear, what our mouths say, and how our emotions respond. We have the ability to monitor ourselves, by the power of God, and to think and act righteously, regardless of circumstances around us. Therefore, it is only when we mimic God's spirit that we will truly move from dust form into spirit form.

Never again allow Satan to deceive you into believing that just because you have experienced some form of dust in your life, this somehow means that you cannot change the form of your entire life. The truth is that you do not have to live in poverty simply because you were born into poverty. You do not have to live under the power of sin just because you were born chained to a sinful existence. You do not have to be an alcoholic just because one of your parents was an alcoholic. You also do not have to settle for a life of dusty, broken dreams just because you were born into a family who lost hope and the ability to dream. The Holy Spirit will give you the power to live above the dust of sin, abuse of alcohol, and broken dreams. God has given us the ability to not only experience a new and more powerful birth, but He has implanted within us a new and powerful spirit-formed life!

Although you began in dust, dust was never meant to be your end!

8

TEN STEPS *to* RISING *from* Life's Ashes

Some of the most beautiful lives are birthed out of the ugliest ashes!

Hello there, you beautiful child of God! Yes, I said that you are beautiful. What? You do not think that you are beautiful just because you have suffered some ashes in your life? Maybe you do not think that you are worth God's time and energy because you were raped. It could be that you have lost a child to drugs, and you are blaming yourself. You might have just suffered from the ashes of a bitter divorce, lost all confidence in yourself and your God, and right now you are feeling ugly inside. Could it be that you had an abortion, and now the guilt is silently killing you? As a result of this, you believe that you are not beautiful. Listen carefully! We might do many things that are downright ugly to God, but that does not mean that the beauty of God is no longer within us. In fact, we might have had the ugliest things done to us and feel like nothing more than a pile of worthless ashes, but God still calls us to the beauty of His Holy Spirit. Therefore, if you have sinned and done something very ugly that God would not approve of, confess that sin unto God and allow Him the opportunity to cleanse you and make you more beautiful than you could ever imagine. God has the supernatural ability to take all the nasty and vile ash within your life and cause the most heavenly and spiritual beauty to rise up from it. Isn't this exciting news?

Now, in order for God to uncover your life from the ashes, He requires you to take some very important steps—ten steps, actually. The first step that you are required to take is to never trust that you are capable enough to handle the ashes in your life. One of the rookie mistakes we make as Christians is to attempt to clean up the ash in our lives by ourselves. We usually do not consult God, and most of the time we end up making an even greater mess. Never attempt to handle an ashy experience by your own intellectual capability because you might get rid of the ash too quickly. You see, sometimes God wants us to grow stronger in His nature, so He allows the ashes of pain, temptation, brokenness, and rejection to stay a bit longer in our lives. Therefore, if we were to quickly remove these ashes, we would be hindering our own spiritual development.

On the other hand, we might end up allowing some ashes to remain in our lives for too long, and this could also be fatal to our faith walk and spiritual development. In fact, we might allow the ashes of bad company, bad habits, and sinful attitudes to stay in our lives beyond their expiration dates, thus giving our lives a very sour and nasty-tasting flavor. Only God truly knows which ashes should be allowed to remain for a time and which should never be allowed back to blacken our most beautiful God-birthed lives. He alone understands what hinders His beauty within us and what promotes His beauty within us. We simply need to allow His Holy Spirit access to our body, soul, and spirit so that He can keep perfect check on everything we allow to enter our life's space. We do this by being open and honest with God concerning everyone that we meet, every feeling that we have, and every thought that we think at that very moment. Even though God already knows all that we think, feel, and everyone we allow into our lives, He does not just push His way into our lives. We must invite Him to enter. Therefore, if you and I will not invite God to handle our ashes for us, He will never enter the private space of our lives and help us. Whenever Jesus Christ came across people with some ash of sickness, sin, or brokenness in their lives, He gently asked them what it was that they wanted before He used His miraculous, ash-clearing touch on them. You see, Jesus already knew what they needed, but He needed them to give Him permission on earth to inject His heavenly power into the ash of their situation. If we do not commit the ashes of our lives unto God, they will bury us!

The second step we need to take is to believe, beyond any doubt, that God has a far greater plan for us than we do. Maybe right now you are wondering how on this earth God could use the ash of your divorce, cancer, rape, or failure in order to bring about anything beautiful or good. God has the ability to take every bad situation in your life and use the ugly ashy results from them to create the greatest beauty. Remember in the book of Genesis how God told Eve, after she had sinned by eating the forbidden fruit, that He would use her womb to help birth a special seed that would crush the serpent's head? God took the ashes of Eve's mistake and decided to use the very womb which brought forth these ashes to cause generations of humankind to be born until Jesus Christ would come and save the world from sin. God is truly magnificent!

Now, if God could do this with Eve, despite her sin, He can surely do the same in your life. All you have to do is believe that God can take the memory of your divorce and use you to give advice to married couples concerning how to avoid divorce themselves. Therefore, your painful divorce does not have to mean the end of your beautiful life in God; rather, it could be a testimony to other married couples about how to preserve their marriage. Isn't it amazing how God can take the ugliness of your divorce and use it to ensure the beautiful continuation of the marital life of another couple? Oh, yes! God has a plan to take the ash of rape in your life and use it as an inspirational book, informing young women how to rise up, even after a rapist has struck them down. Furthermore, God is waiting to get His powerful hands on the ash of your child abuse past. He wants to reveal to others who might have suffered the same agonizing experience that you have, that there is healing available to them. God knows how to take every ash in our lives and cause other people to rise up out of their defeat, even as we also rise.

A third important step is to never allow what you see to cause you to panic. Think about it this way. A speeding car is coming toward you at one hundred miles per hour. You panic and freeze right in its path. Now, what do you think is going to happen? Well, let me tell you the answer. You are going to be killed! This is how it would be if you were to panic in the face of an ash-filled life. When a very bad or painful event happens to us, it is human nature to panic and freeze. However, if we were to continue to live life in this way, we would simply be allowing the ashes of life to roll right over us. If you have failed God by having sex outside of marriage, do not panic or you will end up overwhelmed by the guilt of this sin instead of confessing it to God and allowing Him to wash you all over. If you allow this guilt to continue, you may feel like you do not deserve the love of God and you might be led to believe that God does not want you anymore. Many Christians have abandoned their faith walk because of their first fall into the ash pile of sin. Never panic, no matter how ugly the ash pile might appear! You must always remember that God is not afraid of the ashes in your life, and neither should you be afraid of them. Now I know that some events in your life are very disturbing to the physical eyes, but you have access to the only wise God capable enough to raise you up out of mountains of ash. Therefore, if you lose your job, do not panic! If you find out tomorrow that you have cancer, do not panic! And, even if you are about to lose your house, remain calm! Please understand that whenever God allows ash to be formed in your life, He is preparing to exalt you and usher you into greatness. Therefore, wherever you find ash in your life, just know that the power and purpose of God is not far behind. Ashes are a sign to the true child of God that God is at work!

There is a fourth step in your rise from the ashes. It is the development of a life of praise. Instead of panicking because of the ash in your life, try praising your way through. The Bible informs us to wear praise like a piece of clothing whenever we are going through times of great heaviness or pain. To praise God is to exalt Him and His awesome power far above the lowly ash and dust realities of our lives. When we celebrate God, we are able to tap into heaven in such a way that it would be as if the ashes do not even exist. Oh, yeah! Praise will become the anti-venom and antidote for the poison of the snake bite of ash. An attitude of praise reveals to God that we see Him as the most important person in our ash-filled lives. God loves this kind of attention! Therefore, we sing songs that portray the beauty of God, dance dances that celebrate the true reality of the power of God, and speak words that declare the wonders of God. Then God will come down, His Holy Spirit shall arise, and He will lift us out of the ashes of this present life. Praise is the scent of love that attracts God to us, where He can blow away the ashes from around us. The Bible informs us that God loves the praises of His people so much that He comes to inhabit, or live within, the house of this praise. He will come. He will move. And you will never be the same again. You will rise from the ashes even as your praises rise from you!

Now, the fifth step to rise from the ashes is to never allow the ashes within your life to dictate your destiny. Do not allow negative situations to tell you what you can or can't do. Hey, just because you might have lost your job does not mean that you are worthless or a bum. In Jesus Christ, you are worth more than your last job. A job does not complete you; therefore, the loss of one should never be allowed to make you feel empty. For those of you who might have lost a house, please do not allow this pain to tell you that you will never get another one. Even if you have not handled your money in a godly manner, do not settle for living in that defeat. You need to repent for not using the money God provided wisely, and ask God for His wisdom so that you can be a better steward of His money. Then prepare yourself for a new and better house. If you have been physically abused by a spouse or parent, do not believe that you are doomed to live the life of a victim. You must never let any past or present physical abuse tell you that your life will never be any good.

Do you know who your God is? He is able to cause a beautiful life to rise from an ugly struggle. You need to speak every positive word of God in the Bible over the ashes of your life until you no longer hear the voice of your ashes. Tell your ashes that God can make all things work out for the benefit of your life. Just because you might have committed a crime in the past does not mean that you have to live the life of a criminal. Oh, no! You do not have to become the image of your last sin. I believe that one of the reasons many first-time offenders become lifelong offenders or criminals is because they were never given a chance to be trusted again after their first mistake. If someone had told them that they did not have to let their lives be defined by their first criminal offense and that they could rise from this ashy experience, they might have turned away from the desire to commit the second and third offense. Therefore, do not allow any past failure from any area of your life be the defining mark of your life. Please remember that although ashes are a big part of your life, your life is not ashes!

The sixth step you should take in order to rise from the ashes is to never spend too much time focusing on them. Always remember that the longer you look at anything, the more that thing will impact you. When Eve fell to sin in the Garden of Eden, she gazed at the serpent's face too long and listened too long to the serpent's voice. This allowed Satan enough time to persuade her to eat from the tree from which God had told them not to eat. Let this be a very serious lesson to us today. When we think too much about yesterday's sin without repenting and getting over the guilt of it, we might be persuaded by Satan to simply give up and live in that sin. If we spend too much time looking into the face of an ex-lover, we might be easily moved to resume a violent relationship of which we had long escaped. We might also be persuaded to enter into a sexual relationship of which we have no business partaking. Yes, my friends! The more time we look into the face of life's ashes, the less we spend before the face of God! When we do not spend enough time with God, we become easy prey to the ashy predators of Satan's world order just waiting to pounce on us. Ashes can only convince us that our lives will be nothing if we allow them to speak too often and if we stare at them too long. Therefore, in order to rise above the ashes within your life, you must spend more time in the face and presence of the Holy Spirit than staring into the ugliness of these ashes.

Another danger with looking too long into the face of your ashes is that you will begin to believe what you see. It is a true principle in life that when we look at anything for too long, we tend to believe this is all our lives will ever be and how our lives will end. Therefore, if one of the ashes within our lives happens to be poverty and we look too long into this present reality, we would probably be convinced that this is all our lives will ever be. We then begin to live as though we will never have enough or that we could never be successful. The things which we focus on will eventually determine the way in which we think. The way in which we think, then, will determine how we live. Even though ashes exist, we must not allow ourselves to be moved or conditioned by them.

The seventh step we must take is to develop a constant prayer life. Christians who do not talk with God will probably only hear the negative voice of their ashes. And if their ashes are speaking more and being heard louder than their God, they will never be able to rise above the stronghold of them. Prayer helps silence every negative voice around us and within us by allowing our minds to ascend to the presence of God, thus allowing God's more influential voice to be heard. Prayer gives believers the ability to know which ashes to avoid and which ones to allow. Constant prayer allows our minds to be shaped by what God reveals and not by how the ashes look. Through a life of prayer, doors that have been shut by the ashes of our lives will be reopened by the manifested power of God. When believers walk in the righteousness of God and really pray in faith, no ashes shall remain around them. Prayer awakens the ashes in our lives and then frees us from them, so that they have no power nor control over our destiny. According to the Old Testament history, a king named Hezekiah discovered that he was going to die. He prayed to God to let him live, and God gave him fifteen more years of life. When this righteous king prayed, God lifted him out of the ashes of death. Wow! Please pray! Never stop praying and talking with your Heavenly Father. Wherever you are experiencing ashes in your life, pray heaven down and pray your way out. Your next rise out of life's ashes could be in your next prayer moment. Pray, baby! Pray!

The eighth step that you must be sure to take in order to rise from the ashes of life is to never quit. Do not give up on God or life just because all that you see around you is ash. I want you to know that ashes are designed to try you and test you, in order to get you into God's destined position. You must endure many ashy experiences in this life so that you can develop a very strong character when dealing with the satanic and the demonic. Ashes are not allowed by God to kill the spirit within you, but to kill the fleshy sinful desires which would hinder the nature of God from being seen in you. Please understand that every time you give up because of the ashes, God will allow you to remain in the dust of ashes until you prove that you can endure it and overcome it. One of the reasons we stay buried under many years of ash, as well as many kinds of ash, is because we are quick to quit. When we give up, God has to take us back through the wilderness of ash to prepare us to live above a life of ash. Now, if we are quick to accept ashes and endure them without quitting, then God will allow us to rise above them and rule over everything concerning them. You see, ashes can never rule over you and bury you once you show them that you are not afraid to face them and endure them. It is only when we are not afraid to endure the ashes of this life that we prove to God we are ready to carry His resurrection power into a world contaminated by dust and ashes. Thus, it is only after we rise from our ashes that we can help sinners around us rise from theirs. The serious reality is that the sinners of this world will never be able to rise from their ashes until they see living proof that it is possible to be born into ashes and still rise out of it. Therefore, as we rise from ashes, so might they!

The ninth step is to change our vision. We are going to have to see the ashes, yet not allow this to be where our vision ends. In other words, you might know that you have been afflicted by cancer; however, your vision is not that you will die because of this cancer, but that you will live because of your God. So, although you have seen the doctor's diagnosis concerning the cancer, your vision does not allow you to accept that cancer will be the end of your life. What awesome and influential believers we would be for God if we did not allow the ashes in our lives to contaminate the vision for our lives. Therefore, if your vision is health, sickness will not kill your life. You can handle any ashy condition once your vision is not defeated by it. If you were to get into a terrible car accident and all that you could see was the blood and harm done to you, your car, or another person, you might lose your mind. However, if you focused your attention on your forgiving God and His ability to love you even if you might have caused the accident, then you can make it through this ugly situation as though you never had gotten into it. Oh, yes, vision is everything. Having the best vision in the worst situations will lead to the greatest victories. Therefore, if we are able to develop a vision of victory in the face of the ashes of defeat, we would be able to experience the powerful movement of the Holy Spirit on our behalf.

However, if we cannot develop visionary eyes of faith, then we will never experience any victory of God and will continue to live in the ashes of defeat. The story in the New Testament of the woman with the issue of blood explains that even though she was bleeding internally, she received her healing by Jesus Christ because she had developed a vision of her healing and not of her sickness. In other words, she had visionary sight for her healing and became blind to her sickness. Because of this, she was completely healed and restored. This biblical and historical fact reveals to us that for all those people out there whom God wishes and has plans to heal from their diseases, if they can simply visualize this healing by faith, God can step in and provide them a wonderful miracle.

Now, in the same manner that there exists people whom God has decided to heal, there also exists those whom He asks to endure through some very hard and rough illnesses. For those of you that have been chosen to endure sickness to the end, please know that there is great inspiration from God for you. When you take on a God-birthed vision for this specific situation, you will be able to look past your present pain and see the glorious future hope of God involving your pain-free, new heavenly body. Just ask the Holy Spirit to take your common earth vision, touch it supernaturally, and give you such a vision of life that it would appear to you as though you were not even in that hospital bed or on that dialysis machine. Therefore, even in the most difficult of situations, the will of God is that we approach it with heaven's vision and not with our own. It is only then that we can be healed, should it be His ultimate will for us, or endure a sickness to its very end should this also be His will for us. But know this! In whatever situation that God might require you to be placed, He has already given you a vision beyond the confinement of that thing. If He intends for you to endure the hardships of great poverty and lack, realize that He has already provided a rich vision of how you are to truly see yourself until He returns to take you completely out of this wilderness of testing. Then, for those of you whom God wishes to bring into great provision for life and ministry, all that you have to do is ensure that you are wearing the binoculars of God's vision; and you will be able to grab a hold of all that God has intended in His mercy for you to possess. Oh yes! Making sure that you are living and walking with a God-breathed vision is not just a good thing, but you will find out that it is one of the most essential things to have in heaven or on this earth. Hey, listen! You are only as strong as the kind of vision you have. And you are either a victim or a victor, based upon your vision. Therefore, whatever you see is what you will inevitably be!

Finally, the tenth step that you must take in order to rise from the ashes of life is not to hang out with ashy-minded people. Whether you wish to accept this or not, you have some people in your life space who are not beneficial to your growth or your destiny in God. If you were to examine every relationship that you are currently in, you would probably discover that you have people around you who are quick to say that you cannot own your own business, or that you should date instead of waiting for God to lead a husband directly to you, or that you do not need to pray or praise so much. People in your life who are constantly speaking doubt, fear, and confusion to your mind are usually ashy-minded people. These people are easily led into sin and they make excuses for living in an ungodly manner. They are surely chickens and not eagles! Do you really want to hang out with people who have no vision beyond the poverty that they are in or the brokenness that they are struggling with? Do you really want to expose the visions of God for your life to people who will simply do nothing but discourage them and discourage you? I hope that your answers would be a resounding, "No!" If you are going to experience a resurrection from the ashes, you cannot hang out with people who are comfortable playing in a pile of ashes. There are people who have no problem playing in the ashes of gay experiences, hate, violence, and many other works of ungodliness. Please, if you intend to live a life far above the dust and ash of this ungodly world order, do not have deep friendships with ashy-minded people. You should minister Christ to them, pray for them, and love them with the love of God, but never allow them into the inner courts of your God-birthed life!

I hope that after reading these important steps on how to rise from the ashes of your life, you will never again settle for a life hidden under ashes. Instead, I hope you will endeavor to live your life soaring with spiritual eagles. God has chosen you to never again allow Satan to drag your precious spirit-formed life back down into the ashes from whence you were delivered. Take hold of the garment of the Holy Spirit's power and walk in the invigorating power of God's character so that you can help others in your family or workplace rise from the dead ashes of their sinful, decaying lives. Jesus is on your side. God's Spirit is within you. And a destiny of resurrection and eternal glory awaits your arrival. Go ahead, live ash free and win! You can win, because Jesus Christ has already won!

The presence of ashes does not indicate an absence of life!

9

born small, *designed* TO be GREAT

God always chooses small people to do great things! The accomplishment of great things is not based on your size, but on the size of your God!

"I am too small!" "I am too poor!" "I am too unknown!" "There is no way that I can do that!" "I am not good enough!" "They might not like me!" "I could never be that brave!" These are the words voiced every time God chooses someone to do something that seems bigger than them or beyond their capability. Are you one of these people who cannot believe that God could use you to raise the dead, preach many souls into His kingdom, and bring much-needed aid to those who are in very poor and needy countries? Do you believe that God can use anyone else but you? Well, I have good news for you! God can use anyone and anything to accomplish His will in this earth because God will be performing the work *through* these vessels, not the vessels themselves. Therefore, it is not the size, strength, fame, or wealth of a vessel that will determine how one is to be used. It is by the power of God's Holy Spirit. God is always in search of the weak, rejected, depressed, poor, and unknown people to perform some of His greatest works and miracles. God does this so that at the end of the day, people will know that only God could have done such a great work or miracle.

In the Bible, we see how God used the womb of Eve, the very woman who gave the cursed fruit to her husband to eat, to give birth to a generation of human beings that would, after forty-two generations, birth the Messiah Jesus Christ. It also reveals how God used ravens, selfish birds, to feed His prophet in the wilderness. We also see how God took water from a stone and gave it to the Hebrew people to drink while they were experiencing their wilderness journey. Now, it does not stop here! God also sent His people a thin wafer-like substance, which they called manna, that He released from the sky to them. These are some awesome miracles God performed to carry out His purpose. Think about it! God allows sinful Eve to be a part of the greatest salvation that would ever be known to humankind. Then, He uses selfish ravens, birds that feed off of death and are not known to help support life. How about this move? God uses a hard stone to bring forth water. That alone is scientifically impossible! All these biblical examples are designed to encourage us that if God could use the most unlikely objects and people to do the most extraordinary things, then so too can God use the weakest, poorest, and least-known people among us to bring about the greatest works.

You are never too small or too unknown to be used by God to do something far larger and greater known than you ever were. Yes, it is true! You might have been born into a very poor and insignificant family. You were led to believe that if your family was never good enough to do anything great then neither are you. Maybe you were born into a family where physical or sexual abuse was very real. Because of this, you feel as if you are too dirty or broken for God to use. Or perhaps you have grown up in a family filled with criminals and some who have spent many years in prison. Because of this, you feel that your future is going to be jail and that God would definitely have no greater plan for your life. To all of you, I say, "Get up!" God has a great plan for your very small and insignificant birth! Yes, you may have experienced one or even all of these possible situations mentioned above; however, God has a far greater experience for you. You are exactly the kind of vessel that God is searching for and calling. Bring your weakness, brokenness, poverty, and insignificance, and give it over to God so that He can heal you and remake you for His kingdom work. Do not listen to Satan's lying words! God has room for you, and God has a plan that will be bigger than who or what you are, or where you were born.

I am a living witness of this. God took me as a nobody and made me something more than I could ever have imagined. I was born in the Bahamas into a very poor family. My mother and father did not have much. I remember that sometimes all we had to eat was white rice and butter. We lived in a very small, two-bedroom apartment in the heart of the ghetto. I grew up around drug addicts, AIDS victims, and I was always a step away from using drugs. Many of the young guys that I grew up around were either in jail, coming out of jail, or about to commit a crime and head directly to jail. Sometimes, I would be playing basketball and see a drug addict taking drugs right on the side of a wall by the basketball court. I witnessed guys beaten almost to death and saw others get stabbed with knives. I started school as a B-, sometimes A-, student. When I got to high school and began to be influenced by peer pressure, I became a D-student. Although my father was in the house, he lived as if he were outside of the house, and so I hardly spent time with him. This lack of attention caused me to rebel in attempts to gain his attention. However, I never got it. When I completed high school (which I barely finished), God began to call me to His purpose. After I had given my life completely over to Him, I had such low self-esteem and struggled with depression that I still did not believe that I was even good or worthy enough to have been chosen by God. Sometimes I wondered if God had made some kind of mistake. Now, many years later, God has done such a heavenly makeover with my dusty and ashy earth-based life that I know He can use me, and I now have a God-given purpose. If God can take my old beat-up life, breathe into it, and make it useful to His will, then I am very much persuaded that He can do the same with yours. Please do not give up on life just because you were born too small, think that you are too weak, or believe that you are too unimportant. God wants you! He will take your small and make it do very big things!

At one point in the Bible, when God's people were in need of a ruler to deliver them from the hands of their enemies, God chose a man called Gideon, who was trying to get a bit of food for his family and was hiding out in fear. Even though God found Gideon in a place of fear, God still chose him. He called him a mighty man of valor, even though Gideon appeared to be the opposite. You see, God called Gideon the mighty man of valor that He would make him into; He did not label Gideon what Gideon was at that time. The Bible further reveals that God gave Gideon an army of three hundred and used this very small group to defeat an army of way more than ten thousand. This story is a remarkable revelation to us that God does not need strong people to win a major battle. He can take scared and mentally weak people, add His power to them, and cause them to do more than seemed possible. This story also reveals to us that God can take a very small and insignificant number of soldiers, lend them His strength, and make them far superior than an army physically stronger in numbers than they. If God can do this, think about what God can do with you!

You might be afraid now because fear might run in your family. However, do not run away from that ministry or preaching assignment for which God has chosen you because whatever God chooses, He makes strong and able to accomplish His assignment. Never worry! In fact, please understand that God is responsible for providing the money, spiritual gifts, physical talents, and spiritual vision to the person He chooses in order to accomplish His task. It is not your job to give yourself the power for any God-birthed assignment. So, stop scaring yourself! God has it all under control! Similarly, please do not walk past that management promotion simply because you do not believe that you can handle leadership.

You can take hold of that job, and with the wisdom of God, you could bring new insights for that company's growth. You must remember that your God has solutions for situations which have not yet existed. Surely God can help you become an excellent manager—one capable of handling any and all challenges in business.

Never allow where you were born to dictate what kind of destiny you could or should have. God can make your destiny far greater than the small size of your birth. As Christians, we need to have this truth drilled into our minds because some of us are constantly avoiding greater challenges in church ministry, on our jobs, in our marriages, or in our schools because we believe that we don't have enough knowledge to effectively deal with them. When we have this small vision, we usually end up accomplishing nothing. But that is not all! When we refuse to believe that God can use us for greater things, we miss out. God will find a person who is not stronger than us but simply believes more than we do to accomplish the task. Do not be replaced! Never allow fear and doubt to cause you to miss out on God's strength and thus to miss some of God's greatest movements! Please know that if you are alive today, God has a specific design for you. He wants to take your small, frail frame and give you His form so that you will effectively carry out His agenda.

You must cast down ignorant words spoken by ignorant people, telling you that you are not good enough or that you have the wrong gender for the job. There are some people who are Satan's spokespeople, designed by him to convince you that your life is worth nothing to God and that you do not even deserve to live. In order for you to receive God's great power and operate in God's great plan, you have to get rid of big talkers who are full of small talk. Even in your family, some are talking loudly, but they are telling you things which make you feel smaller than you really are. They are predicting a future for you that God does not intend for you. Be careful of people who tell you what they think you are or what they think you can and cannot do, but they have neither consulted nor heard from God the truth of all that He is going to make you. Some friends around you are speaking very negative things to you and about you because they are jealous of the potential they see in you. You must never seek to define yourself, and neither should you let anyone else define you, by their words. No one else knows the plans God has for you, and He doesn't reveal them to just anybody. Therefore, do not be quick to come into agreement with anyone's beliefs concerning what God will do with your life.

In fact, you must never even trust that *you* know all that God can make of you, because even your best guess is far from

God's truest reality of what you are meant to do and accomplish. Most of the time, our own vision of what we can truly become has been tainted by our own failures, insecurities, and negative thoughts. Therefore, how we see ourselves is not how God sees us! God looks past our last sin and sees a Christian who can overcome sin. He looks past our fears and sees a bold soldier ready for the fight. God is also able to look past our lack of self-esteem, and He sees a faith-filled believer. Therefore, when God speaks to us, He speaks to our present state of "can't do" from the future place of "already done." We can be encouraged in knowing that the things which we think we cannot handle, through God, we have already handled them! You can do and become all that God says you can do and become because He will make it so.

There are some people in this life who never get into position with God to accomplish great things because they spend their entire lives believing that they have no worth. These people have allowed the wrong words, misguided people, and bad events to cause them to only see themselves as victims and not victors. As a matter of fact, you and I might know people like this. We might be friends, family, or even spouses of these people. If this is the case, we have an obligation by God to inform them that they can be more than they know. We must tell them that they do not have to live like this and that God has more for them. Please let us pray that they become what God has designed and not just settle for living in the way that they were born.

Never live small again! Once God has touched your life, you have become more than you were at birth. Jesus has given you an experience which the human womb could not release to you, and now you carry God's life on the inside of you. How dare you live small! Live big! In God, you are bigger than how you see yourself, and you can do far greater things than the limited size of your mind. Therefore, let your very huge God live very big through you, and let this small-minded world of humankind bow down to His awesome greatness!

10
Ruling over dust, BREAKING UGLY addictions

We can never truly love ourselves until
we learn to hate our addictions!

I see you. I see your pain as you fight and fight against the passionate inner demons within your life. You are so tired of having to crawl back on your knees to God for forgiveness after telling yourself that you would never commit that sin again. It seems like the more you strive to get on top of this beast within, the more you fall under the ugly weight of this hidden shame. Oh yes, I know you. I know you because I was you. I know what it is to love God but to also secretly struggle with addictions that are totally against the will of my God. I understand the conflict of desiring to touch God and grow in

His Spirit, while still wanting to hold onto things that are purely of a flesh nature. Yes indeed, I feel your pain! I hear your inner spirit crying out every time you watch that movie you know you should not be watching. I also hear the screams of your soul as you cannot seem to let go of that sexual relationship you know is leading you down to the pit of sin and shame. I hear you, but most important, God sees you!

It is amazing how the desires of this present world get underneath the skin of our life and become the chains of our souls. You see, the more we become involved in things of the flesh, the more we end up desiring them. Soon, our desire to have them becomes our addiction. Once this happens, we find ourselves hooked to things which often hinder our relationship with God. An addiction is the state in which the things that we once ruled are now ruling us. Think about it. People who start smoking usually start with just one cigarette and are able to smoke that one without needing ten more. However, after smoking this one cigarette, they soon increase to smoking two packs a day. Suddenly, they cannot stop themselves and are being controlled by the very cigarette they could once control. Now isn't this a sad situation? In an addictive state, we permit our addictions to speak to us, instead of us speaking to them. When we allow addictions to tell us how much we should eat, watch, or drink, we have truly crossed the line from being in control to them being in control.

Addictions are very strong ties to physical things in this earth. When we are addicted to anything, this means that our soul (mind, emotions, and will) has been completely overpowered by the taste, touch, smell, sound, and attractiveness of those addictions. In other words, addictions come from things that we have come to enjoy tasting, touching, smelling, hearing, and seeing. Please be aware that the process that has brought us to the ugly place of addiction has found a way to get us to literally love it. Oh yes! We usually love the things we are addicted to. Can you imagine that? Although the nicotine within every cigarette is really slowly killing us, we still love it. Even though having illicit and unprotected sex outside of marriage can cause sexually transmitted diseases, people still love to do it because it feels so good. Therefore, we often fall in love with the very things that are killing us! The power of addictions exists because, although we know it is so wrong, it is difficult to loose ourselves from it because it feels so right! When we allow ourselves to be governed by our human emotions or feelings, we become addicted to the most horrible things. Our feelings betray our very lives and, like Judas, take us down into tombs of death and suck the very potential of God right out of us.

Since you know that we can become addicted to many things, you should also realize that we can get the control back. Think about it! The reason for an addiction in our life is because we have given that thing permission to operate within our lives. Now, if we can give a thing permission in our lives, then we can also give God permission to break its power and hold from our lives. Oh yes, you can gain control over your life by yielding your addicted life over to a power and presence far greater than your addictions. Only God has enough power to overpower and control all the things which have been controlling your life. The good news is that God wants to enable you to rule yourself, but you must allow Him complete control over you.

In the book of Genesis, God told Cain that sin wanted to rule him but that he should rule it instead. You see, God wants to grant you the authority to say no to that cocaine addiction or that nicotine craving. God gives us the power to say *yes* to the things that are good for us and *no* to the things that are no good for us. God wants us to rule over the dusty and ugly addictions in our lives so that we might show off His awesome dominion in heaven and earth. He wants to use and empower us to cast out our inner addictive demons so that sinners would know that there is hope for them. God wants sinners to know that they do not have to live with or under the demonic-controlled addictions of this world order and that through His Holy Spirit, they can truly be free. Only when we have learned to hate and dominate our own addictions will the helpless and powerless others around us truly see that the power of God can break any and all addictions. Thus, there are people waiting for you to allow God to crush the head of your addictions so that they could be delivered from theirs.

Maybe you are wondering how you could possibly break an addiction that has controlled your family for many years. You must be thinking that if your great-grandfather could not break it and your daddy surely did not break it, then how could you even begin to overcome this hideous beast within. Well, I will simply tell you that there is no addiction known to humankind that can stand up to the awesome power of God. No way in heaven! Therefore, the first thing you need to do to break every ugly addiction in your life is to let go. Let go of the control of your life and let God take the steering wheel. It is only when you give God your complete self, the good and the bad, that He is able to remove the poisonous addictions which have been such an inborn ugliness in your life. You should know that two masters can never be in control of your life at the same time. This cannot happen because your mind was designed to be controlled by only one influence at a time. Therefore, if two masters were to control your mind at the same time, you would suffer a mental overload and neither of them would be able to use your life for any one particular purpose. This is the reason Jesus told us that we could never serve two masters. In the same way that it is impossible for a human body to play two sports at the same time, so is it impossible for one mind to respond to two competing thoughts at the same time. The more you commit your weaknesses to God by devoting your mind to prayer, the more God will commit His strength to you. God will only transfer and commit His addiction-breaking strength to us when we yield ourselves to His total control. Thus, those whom God is allowed to control will never have to live under the control of any addiction. Give God complete control and then your life will never be lived out of control!

The second requirement for breaking every ugly addiction in your life is to not give in. Now I know this is easier said than done, but if God's power and anointing is already alive within you, then you have the strength not to give in. Please understand that the more you and I give in to any addiction, the more control that it will have over us. Thus, the more I smoke, the more I am going to want to continue to smoke. The more that I drink, the more I am going to remain a slave to the bottle. Oh, yes, an addiction knows that the more it is loved, the more control it is going to have. So, we must break the strength of this addiction by not giving into its pull. Now, this is going to be one of the greatest pains that you will ever experience in your entire life. The length of time you have been controlled by an addiction will determine the level of pain that you will have to endure. Although it was easy giving into the sweet taste of that cigarette, it is going to feel like labor pains when you decide not to give in to this sweet but deadly pleasure. Oh no! It is not easy letting go! However, if Jesus endured the far greater pain of the cross for our sins, then surely we can bear the pain of breaking a very bad and nasty habit so that He can be revealed through our addiction-free lives!

The third thing we must do to break free from the ugly addictions in our lives is to come face to face with the end result of this addiction. In order to want to break the hunger for nicotine, one simply needs to visit the cancer ward in any hospital and see the damage that cigarette smoking causes to the lungs and the body. Sometimes coming face to face with the damage caused by an addiction can cause one to develop a fear for allowing the continuation of that addiction. In Ecclesiastes 7:2, the Bible informs us that it is good for a person to spend time visiting the dead in order to gain a better perspective on the importance of life. You see, the worst thing we can do when trying to gain power over any addiction is hide our faces from the terrible end result. An addiction will always have power over us when we continue to see it as something beautiful and sweet. It is only when we visit the death that this addiction may bring that we will truly be inspired to break its hold over our destiny. Please do not run away from the ugliness that an addiction might produce in your life, or you may never escape this addiction or the potential death that comes with it. Crush the head of the snake of any addiction by not hiding your eyes from the horrible sting it brings.

The fourth action you must take in stopping any addiction dead in its tracks is to fast. Jesus once told His disciples that fasting helps to kick some things out of a person's body (Matt. 17:21). Fasting means to withhold or to go without. Therefore, when breaking an earth-based pleasure, you are going to have to break your appetite for that thing. If we would refrain from giving our body everything that it wants, then we would truly live free. If we want to break the lust for food which manifests itself in the sin of gluttony or greed, then we are going to have to withhold our mouths from food. If we are going to break free from watching pornographic movies, then we have to stop feeding our eyes and ears this pleasure. If we starve our desire for anything, then we will inevitably starve the power of the addiction itself. Thus, fasting allows us to put aside lesser desires and develop a more potent hunger for greater things. The more we go without the physical things of this world, such as food, television, and shopping, the more time we would have to give ourselves over to prayer, fasting, walking with God, and being witnesses of Jesus' life and resurrection. If we keep our minds on the greater things above, then we can starve ourselves of the nasty addictions here below. Is it better to have our hearts filled with all that is of God's Spirit or to have our human bodies filled with all that is satanic and dead?

The fifth course of action you must take to break the control of any addiction is to never hang out with people who have learned to love their addictions. There is a classic principle in this life that if you intend to soar with eagles, you cannot be found hanging around with turkeys. The more you hang out with people who do not want to be freed from alcohol addiction, the closer to impossible it will be for you to reject the abuse of the bottle. If you continue to be close with sexually addicted people, then you will never be able to experience a life of great value that is freed from seeking value through many sexual conquests. We usually become just like the people with whom we associate. Oh, yes, indeed! You can never truly break any addiction while hanging around people who refuse to allow God to break theirs. Therefore, if your overweight problem stems from an out-of-control eating habit, then you are going to have to get your appetite under control. If you are going to bring your appetite under control, then you cannot hang around people who are gluttons. Thus, in order to break an addiction, you have to break away from those who refuse to become untied from that same addiction. Allow God to lead you to relationships that are of His choosing.

God will put people in your life who have been addicted like you, but who refused to live an addicted life. These are the kinds of people you need to be around. It is unwise to place your life in the hands of anyone who can only remind you of your addicted past; they will only make you want to live there again. You must be around people who serve as powerful testimony of a God-centered and addictive-free future. This will afford you every opportunity to want to live free and be free. You see, we want to be freed from an addiction when we become zealous to be like others who have already tasted this God-breathed freedom. Thus, if you want to rise above the dust of addictive decay, you must be prepared to do everything demanded of you by God in order to never be like dust again. Change your relationships and change your destiny.

The sixth thing you should do to break every one of life's ugly addictions is to change your pursuit. If the truth be told, one of the many reasons we became addicted to a thing in the first place is because we ran after or pursued it. Think about this! We would not have become chain smokers had we not pursued that first smoke. We would not have become sexual addicts if we had not pursued that first kiss, which led to that first touch and then, inevitably, to that first sexual encounter. Therefore, if we had run away from addictive substances or lifestyles, instead of toward them, we would be free today. Now, this leads me to the opinion that those things we pursue can become the very things that enslave our hearts and contaminate our spirits. So, if we want to reverse this reality, we have to change our pursuit. If we chase after God's words found in the Bible, we will fill our minds with good addictive thoughts and not harmful ones. This, in turn, would help us create positive addictive actions that will change people's lives for the better. When we place all our energies into developing an addictive prayer life, then we will learn how to live as spiritual predators against worldly addictions, instead of being prey for every filthy, addictive act in this life. When our pursuit is the will of God, then our future's outcome can only be very bright, successful, and victorious. Thus, if our pursuit of the wrong things brings us into bondage, then our pursuit of the right things sets us free. Pursue God, and you will live above the dirt of ugly addictions.

The seventh action required of you is the development of a no-tolerance attitude. Never get to the place in your life that you begin to make excuses for your addictions. If you do this, you are indirectly telling addictions that there is room for any and all of them in your life. In fact, we are usually addicted to the things for which we make the most allowances, and we usually make the most allowances for the things for which we make the most excuses. You see, if I have an eating problem and I keep telling myself that it is okay for me to eat without any limitations because my entire family eats this way, then I am setting myself up for a food addiction because I have tolerated this very harmful behavior with my own words. Please, take care! We often give power to very dangerous things simply because we do not develop a no-tolerance attitude toward them. God will not stop the addictions from operating within our lives if we choose to sit back and tolerate them.

The New Testament informs us that Jesus told His disciples that God would only bind or loose the things that they would bind (disallow) or loose (allow) on this earth. What Jesus was making very clear to these guys was that if they were to sit back and allow evil to happen in their lives, then He would allow it to continue. However, if they were to make a stand against wicked works, then He would stand with them against such works of evil. Thus, if we tolerate addictions within our lives, we leave no room for God to break them off. However, if we do not tolerate any kind or level of addiction, then God will not allow this addiction to wreak havoc in our lives. Take note! Only that which we tolerate can truly be addictive to us! Thus, do not sit back and allow yourself to eat the entire house and the kitchen sink, and do not accept the lie that your body was made to be another person's play toy. Rise up out of the dust. With the power of God's weapons, gifts, and character, fight against every filthy and ungodly thing that is designed to sabotage you and make you a mere walking addict. God has intended better and much loftier things for your life.

Well, by now you understand not only that addictions *can* be broken but, most important, *how* they can be broken. Therefore, do not live only to die as an addict. Live by the Spirit of God, so as to make other addicts believe that they were born to be more than they are right now. Live and move as an addict, hooked on the sweet nectar of all that is God, and watch all other weaker and lesser addictions become nothing but shadows of the past and mere dusty memories of the mind. You are destined to be more! God has ordained you to be more! How can you now ever settle for being anything less?

We can never truly rule over any addiction until we break it, and we can never break any addiction until we learn how to rule it!

GOD'S *Masterpiece*

A BEAUTIFUL PICTURE OF GOD REMAKING YOU

What life's hardships have made ugly,
God is well able to make beautiful!

There is no doubt that we were all born into an ugly world and surrounded by very ugly circumstances. In fact, even when a baby is being birthed, the pain the mother has to endure is so harsh and cruel that it is a sign of the ugliness the baby will one day face in the future as an adult. Additionally, if you were to look at a newborn baby, just pushed out of the womb, the beauty of the baby is hidden by so much blood that the ugliness of this blood might just startle you. Now, if life begins with the experience of ugliness in labor pain, think about how ugly life can become or end if God were not present to intervene and change this messy experience and outcome. Oh, yes, thank God for Jesus Christ, who is able to bring heaven's beauty into our ugly and traumatized lives.

All of us have gone through or will go through some very ugly circumstances designed by Satan to either destroy us before we accept Jesus as Lord, or to defeat God's potential within us after we have accepted Jesus Christ as our Savior. Some people have been made ugly by drug addiction. This addiction has so disfigured their minds and emotions that they can't even live one day without tasting this destroyer of any beauty in their lives. Then there are some people who have been ravaged by the abuse of alcohol, and their lives have no greater pleasure than that of the very bottle that is killing them. There are also those who have been battered and physically abused, left scarred for life by some abusive spouse. They are so disfigured by this abuse that they do not believe they can find love or even be loved. They are hurting, and no amount of psychological counseling seems to be working. Oh, yes, there are some precious lives out there who have endured or passed through so much ugliness that they believe they will never see beauty again. Some of them have even attempted suicide because of the pain and agony of very brutal and ugly experiences. Despite all this ugliness, I wish for you to know that there is a very beautiful God that is about to make a beautiful masterpiece out of the ugliness of your life.

From the book of Genesis, the first book of the Bible, we get a clear picture of the fact that God is always creating. This wonderful chapter in the Bible's written history reveals that there is no beauty without God; in fact, there is no life to beautify without God. God shows us through the physical creation of the world that He is well able to take the ugliness of any life and make it into a beautiful masterpiece. If we follow the creative process over the seven days of creation, we would discover just how God takes a life from the reality of nothingness and forms it into something both beautiful and purposeful. Once we release the brokenness of our lives to God, He will take our broken pieces and make a wonderful vessel, worthy of His use and useful for His purpose. Only God can take the ugliness of a drug-scarred, physically abused, depression-riddled, and poverty-stricken life and change it to a life that will make people go, "Wow!" God can so transform a seemingly insignificant life into one so significant and beautiful that it would be as if the life always were that way. God can so restore our lives that it would be as if we were never broken! Now that is awesome!

Let's discuss how God transforms broken and messed-up lives into lives that are amazing masterpieces. When God began to create everything in the biological and physical world, He started with the state of nothingness. There was nothing in existence except the awesome presence and power of our self-existent God. God is so powerful that all that He needs to form and shape great beauty is Himself. He does not require help from anything or anyone; He is completely and solely God! Now, when God begins to work on your life, He discovers you in the place of being nothing and having nothing. This means that you were born, but you had no fellowship with Him; you had no righteousness in and of yourself; you had no right to God's heavenly peace; and you did not have any living spiritual beauty within yourself. Therefore, although you truly were alive on this earth, heaven counted you as dead before God placed His beautiful, created spirit within you. Be encouraged that if you have no money in your life, if you have lost friends and confidants, or if you feel you have been brought down to a place of nothingness, God is able to make you complete and fulfilled.

God loves to find us in the state of nothingness. Then, when people see the end result of fantastic beauty in your life, they will never be able to say that it is because of you. Think about this! All God wants you to do is to give your non-righteous life to Him and let Him make it righteously beautiful. God wants you to give your non-confident life to Him, and watch Him fill you with His Holy boldness. Then, God wants you to give Him your lack of money experience and watch Him give you a miracle of His wisdom to make you financially full and satisfied. Give all your nothing to God and watch Him make you more than you ever were and give you more than you ever had! God took the nothingness in the book of Genesis and, when He had finished, the most wondrous and beautiful things were made and are still alive today, by the power of His Holy Spirit and His holy, living Word. Cheer up! God has a very magnificent plan for your nothing-filled life. Trust Him! He knows what to do with the nothingness surrounding you!

Now, nothingness was not the only thing that God encountered while creating the masterpiece of the universe. According to Genesis, God had to deal with the reality that after He had begun to create, creation still had no form and was empty, or devoid, of life. The formlessness at the beginning of the creative process meant that, although creation had begun, there was no ability to support life. This is exactly what happens in our lives. Although we are physically born, our lives have no form of godliness and no form of spiritual vision. In other words, even though we are living, we are not living to perfection nor are we living up to the full standard of God's excellence. We have a human shape that is out of shape because it cannot yet hold the presence of God and neither can it fulfill God's destiny. In truth, we were without form. We also had a life that was empty, void of substance. We were empty of God's vision, power, eternal life, and spirit nature. Once we accepted Jesus Christ as Lord, He gave us spiritual form and fullness. These two awesome gifts gave us access to carry God's breath, life, and power. We also have the ability to release God's spiritual life from within us because we are now filled up with the Holy Spirit.

Even though we have an awesome form from God and are filled with His wonderful nature, sometimes in our God-led lives we are going to have moments in which we still feel unformed and empty. Sometimes you and I are going to look at our bank accounts and see no form of money, only an empty account. In other cases, we are going to have no form of friends around us to help or encourage us. There are times that we will be empty of human networks that can give us aid or assistance. Now, if you are God's child and you feel this way, it does not mean that you are completely without form or that your God-birthed new life is completely empty. Oh no! Even though He has truly formed us and filled us, God allows some parts of our past formlessness and emptiness to continue to challenge us in present times. This helps us never forget that it is Him who has given us form and fullness and not our human friendships nor network connections. God wants the praise and boasting to be given to Him alone. In addition, God wants us to never become satisfied in staying with our level of spiritual growth; He wants us to be discomforted so we continue to chase after Him for greater levels of spiritual form and fullness. These are the reasons we sometimes feel as if we have not truly escaped from our former life of formlessness and emptiness. Therefore, when you get to the place, after experiencing such a well-formed and full life of God, that you see yourself as formless and empty, do not panic! Go into prayer and praise and watch God take you to a greater level of His form and fullness. Believe me, He will!

As God continued His creative process, according to the book of Genesis, He encountered darkness. Now, this darkness was at first a physical one, in which there existed no light or even light energy. In the midst of this darkness, God called light into being, and the darkness had to fall away and allow God's light to have complete authority. When God first found us, we were born into, and lived surrounded by, a very different kind of darkness. This darkness was a spiritual one, filled with all kinds of dark sins, wickedness, and evil practices. We were completely blinded to the reality of God and to His pure righteous light. We were doomed to fail and to fall into the satanic pits of this unholy world order. However, Jesus entered our dark and gloomy existence, gave us God's light, and released to us God's true vision of what we should be and how we were expected to live.

Although this is a wonderful truth, it does not mean that we will never experience some form of darkness test ever again. Oh no! As long as we live in this dark and satanic world, we will be tested by temptations which try to get us to live in darkness once more. In fact, you might be going through some kind of temptation at this very moment. Maybe you are battling some deadly disease or you are being revisited by an ex-lover. You might be tempted to steal money from your job because you have fallen on some dark, financially lacking times. Do not let the darkness, no matter what it might be, cause you to doubt that God is still working on you and making you into a beautiful masterpiece. The mere fact that darkness is still around you only serves to reveal that God is very much at work within you. Please remember that God does His most beautiful work in the ugly state of the most blinding darkness. Think about it! God found you in darkness and did not give up on you. Do you now think that just because a little darkness has entered your life, God will abandon you? God is definitely not finished with you. Never mind the darkness; all you need to do is continue to walk toward God's light! God is making you a wondrous work of light art.

As God began in Genesis to face all this formlessness, emptiness, and darkness around Him, He did not panic. In fact, Scripture further reveals that He simply went into a state of rest or calm. Now, if God does not panic in the face of all this negativity, then you should never panic because you are seated in Him. Since you are now born of God and if you have been baptized into the Holy Spirit of His power, you do not need to be scared when you encounter the realities of formlessness, emptiness, and darkness. You just need to sit back, relax in praise and prayer, and allow the Holy Spirit to make you beautiful. Remember, you are not responsible for making yourself spiritually beautiful; God is the master artist who is responsible for all and any beauty in your life. Therefore, if God relaxes in difficult times, then you just need to relax with Him. God has you covered!

Furthermore, as God continued to create beauty in the face of overwhelming ugliness in the book of Genesis, He created light without the sun. When God commanded light to exist, it did not come from the sun. This light was simply the essence of illumination that is light. This was an awesome miracle since it is impossible to get light without the sun as the source of light. However, this is God at work! God can give you one million dollars without the source—the bank. In other words, God can take the impossible ugliness in your life and cause great beauty to appear, even where there is no physical source of beauty. This also demonstrates that God does not need you to already have beauty in order to make you beautiful. He will simply take the beauty out of Himself, just as He did with the creation of light, and make you more beautiful than anyone attempting to be beautiful with every substance in this present world. All of this information continues to prove that your true and real beauty is spiritual and that it can only be found in and produced by God.

As we look further into the book of Genesis in chapter 1, we see how God placed a dividing line in the midst of the oceans below and the sky above. This invisible line was used to separate and reveal to us the two kinds of water which are a vital part of this planet. On the one hand, you have the waters in the sky in the form of vapor. Then, there exists the waters below the dividing line and the sky, which we have come to know as the oceans and seas. Now, there is an awesome revelation in this concerning how God remakes us. Whenever God is remaking us, He not only gives us access to all the resources of heaven, but He also grants us access to the resources of earth. In other words, He gives us two kinds of beauty. He gives us the ability to get money from banks that would never grant us loans because of our bad credit and high debt. However, He may choose another way and cause money to come directly from heaven through the mouth of a fish perhaps, even as He did for the disciples in the New Testament. God can provide us with the goods on earth, but, when these waters suffer drought, He is able to release spiritual waters from heaven. This is how God gave His people bread from heaven and water from out of a rock. Never panic! When God allows the physical waters of earth's beautiful resources to fail you, then He will open up the windows of heaven and pour out on you so much supernatural water that He could make a new ocean in your world and life. God is also revealing that your beauty is never limited to earth, but is limitless because of the waters above or in the heavenly regions. Therefore, whenever God is remaking you, He gives you a beauty that cannot be limited by this world's ugliness. What an awesome heavenly makeover!

Genesis chapter 1 continues to reveal a beautiful picture of how God will remake your life when it explains how God separated dry land from the depth of the oceans and seas. This means that when God is bringing you into His ordained beauty, He will deliver you from all the ugliness that has been seeking to drown your life. Oh, yes, there are some very satanic and ugly plans to sink your life and drown every God-designed purpose for your life. I believe that Satan will send oceans of sickness, distress, sin, temptation, pain, depression, and doubt so that your soul would be overwhelmed and your spirit would never rise again. However, God knows how to part deep waters, as in the parting of the Red Sea, and bring you out on dry ground. God will deliver you out of deep and ugly oceans by remaking your life in such a way that no satanically created ocean would be able to drown your faith, purpose, and God-breathed design. Isn't it powerful to know that your heavenly makeover enables you to float and even walk on the waters of deep, dark, ugly oceans of sin. Yes, my friend, you do not have to live a drowning or sinking life! The remade beauty of God in you makes you the master of life's deepest oceans. Therefore, when God is remaking you, He gives you dry ground in your life so you can bring other struggling and drowning people to God's safe place. God never allows deep oceans to enter your life's space without first giving you heaven's dry land. In fact, the beauty of God in us is that for every ocean of trouble, stress, and pressure in our lives, we have God's dry ground. God makes you able to live above the swelling tides of such ugliness. When God remakes you, you can swim and never sink because He gives you the power to sail over the most dangerous seas of demonic influence.

We also see a picture of how God remakes a person's life, when we look at how He creates every kind of seed-bearing tree. God created trees that would feed the man He would soon create, and He made trees which would one day help heal physical illnesses that man would develop because of his do it! Do not be afraid. Your life is not truly over unless you stop sowing the seeds of your God-birthed makeover. Never stop sowing!

As we continue through Genesis chapter 1, we witness the creation of the controlling elements for the light He had made. God made the sun to control the daytime light. He then made the moon to control the light at night and the stars to assist with the moon's light. These objects are very important. The sun produces the light necessary for energy and continuous birthing of life. Since we cannot do without light, the moon draws from the sun's light at daytime to transfer light to us during the night. The stars are the go-between light, which sailors use to chart courses by night and sail ships to their correct ports of call. This awesome creative sophistication expresses that when God remakes any life, He places within it a light that can reproduce itself for those who are in sinful darkness. God remakes your life, like the moon, to take His beautiful light and give it to those who are living and suffering in the darkness of their burdensome night. Then, God gives those remade lives the ability to be like the stars. They are able to direct the lost sinners of this world into His kingdom for salvation and life eternal. God is always trying to make dim lives into bright stars that will show the way back to Him and His loving heart. Do you not know that you are designed by

God to be a carrier of His beautiful light? God does not make people into darkness; He transforms them into both brilliant light *and* carriers of light.

We also see that God made man in His image and likeness. God created a creature of flesh designed to carry His Spirit's breath and control the earth on His behalf. The words *image* and *likeness* meant that this first human being was to operate like God and live as a representative of the invisible God. In other words, God remakes people to walk in His character and demonstrate His reality and will. God remakes you to follow His pattern of living, to walk in His plans for your life, and to show others how to follow after Him. Therefore, God expects us to tell the truth because He is truth. He wants us to live in love because He is love. God requires that we abstain from sex outside of marriage, because He designed the sexual experience to be between one man and one woman in marriage. Whatever the Bible reveals to us about God is the way we are to live. Being made in the image and likeness of God means that we can live a life of holiness. We can live above the addictions of drugs, alcohol, sex before marriage, and pornography. The beauty of how God remakes a person is that He causes that person to no longer be a slave to sin. Thus, God is not making slaves; He is in the business of making sons. God, like any human father, wants to reproduce His image into the lives of His children. Then, when they are seen, people will be able to see God's face in them.

Well, we have come to the final creation of God in the book of Genesis. Now, I know that Bible scholars have long believed that God finished creating on the sixth day. This is believed because Genesis says that God rested on the seventh day. When we think of God resting, we think of Him as neither working nor creating. However, we would be very misguided. The mere fact that God rested on the seventh day, means that He created rest. Oh, yes! God created the state of rest. What this means to those of us who are going through the process of God's greatest makeover is that we have been given the greatest rest in existence—God's eternal rest. This kind of rest can never be disturbed, nor can it be overwhelmed by any storm. This is the kind of rest that allowed Jesus to actually sleep through the noise of a super storm. God has given us this kind of rest so that when Satan's storms arise in our lives, we will never be blown away by fear. When the windy storms of sickness and mental suffering come, recognize that you have been given God's rest so you can sleep right through to the end of them. Please understand that storms are a part of life, but the rest of God can withstand them all. So, be thankful for the way God has remade you. God has remade you to endure until

Jesus comes to rapture you out of this planet. God's rest in your made-over life is exactly what you need in order to kiss the face of every storm and survive its breath!

I hope that the information in this God-revealed and inspired book would be of great help and encouragement to your life. God wants you to know that He makes nothing ugly, even though He might allow ugliness to happen to a life. He simply wants to collect all the dust and ugliness of your life, breathe into it, and make something new and living out of it. God also wants you to know that He will continue to take that which has been rendered useless, apply His touch, and make it of great use for His purpose and plan for your life. Thus, it is with these last words that I wish you God's success, breath, and victory in this life and in the next. God bless you and your entire families. May you increase in God as you decrease in yourself!

---

*Whatever God is making you, no one,
including yourself, has ever seen!*

About the Author

Apostle Kevin A. Johnson is a born-again worshipper of God. He is a native of the Bahamas and is the son of the late Samuel Johnson and Ms. Maud Dorcas Stubbs. Apostle Johnson is married to the former Terrah L. Rolle, and together they have been blessed with five beautiful and anointed children—Zoe, Rachel, Sarah, Benjamin, and David. Apostle Johnson lives in Nashville, Tennessee and is the senior apostle and president of Breathe Again Ministries. He and his wife are the God-appointed leaders of a local and international conference-style ministry. Apostle Johnson believes that God, by His Holy Spirit, has given spiritual gifts and physical talents to His people of faith. However, it is the responsibility of these people of faith to use His gifts and talents for the express purpose of promoting the Gospel of Jesus Christ, strengthening the Church, and impacting the sinful world with the miraculous power of God. According to Apostle Johnson, these spiritual gifts and physical talents should not be used for the promotion of human egos nor for making God's servants into objects of worship. His spiritual philosophy can be summed up in this simple but powerful statement: In order for any life to have a good end, it must be lived by and through the power and presence of the Holy Spirit!

Should you wish to reach Apostle Kevin A. Johnson for special prayer, counseling, conferences, or revivals, please feel free to contact him at (615) 916-9479 (mobile) or email him at apostlekaj@yahoo.com or ale18@tmo.blackberry.net.